Wakefield Press

The Missing Photograph

Christopher Race published short stories in the 1980s before taking a BA degree at The University of Melbourne. His career has been that of an editor and writer, working in London as a copywriter before returning to Melbourne and working as Editorial Manager for the Australian internet search engine, LookSmart Intl.

He worked as a freelance editor while at RMIT University gaining his Grad. Dip. Info Management to become a librarian in 2008. He has held positions in Melbourne and Central Victoria.

More recently Christopher Race has being writing and publishing poetry both as an author, *Still Life With Grandmother*, 2015, and as an editor for *Shots from the Chamber*, 2016.

Since 2016 he has been writing prose including *The Missing Photograph*.

The Missing Photograph

Christopher Race

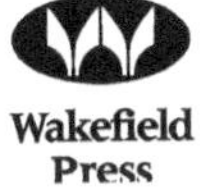

Wakefield
Press

Wakefield Press
16 Rose Street
Mile End
South Australia 5031
www.wakefieldpress.com.au

First published 2025

Picture credits
Chs 1, 4, 10, 11, 12, 13, 15, 17, 19, 20, 21 – the author
Ch 2 – J Nicholls
Ch 6 – NASA
Ch 8 – P Bruegel
Ch 14 – B Nicholls, C More
Chs 3, 5, 7, 22 – Unknown

Text designed and typeset by Jesse Pollard, Wakefield Press

ISBN 978 1 92338 804 8

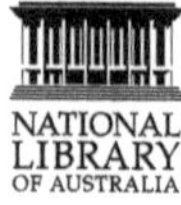

A catalogue record for this book
is available from the National
Library of Australia

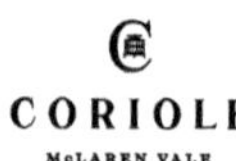

Wakefield Press thanks
Coriole Vineyards for
continued support

Contents

1	Couple in Suburban Civic Garden	1
2	Vacant Block	7
3	Two Young Men Smoking	13
4	Arthropod	21
5	A Family Outing	29
6	Saturn by Cassini	37
7	Yorkshire Shopfront	43
8	*Landscape with the Fall of Icarus* – Bruegel	49
9	What is a Photograph?	56
10	Young Woman	61
11	Storm Cloud	67
12	Two Old Friends	73
13	Five Pieces of Fruit	81
14	Destiny	87
15	Self-Portrait	95
16	The Missing Photograph	101
17	The Creek	109
18	Three Images Remembered	115
19	Landscape	123
20	Beatrice	129
21	The Madame Alfred Carrière Rose	137
22	The Gate	147

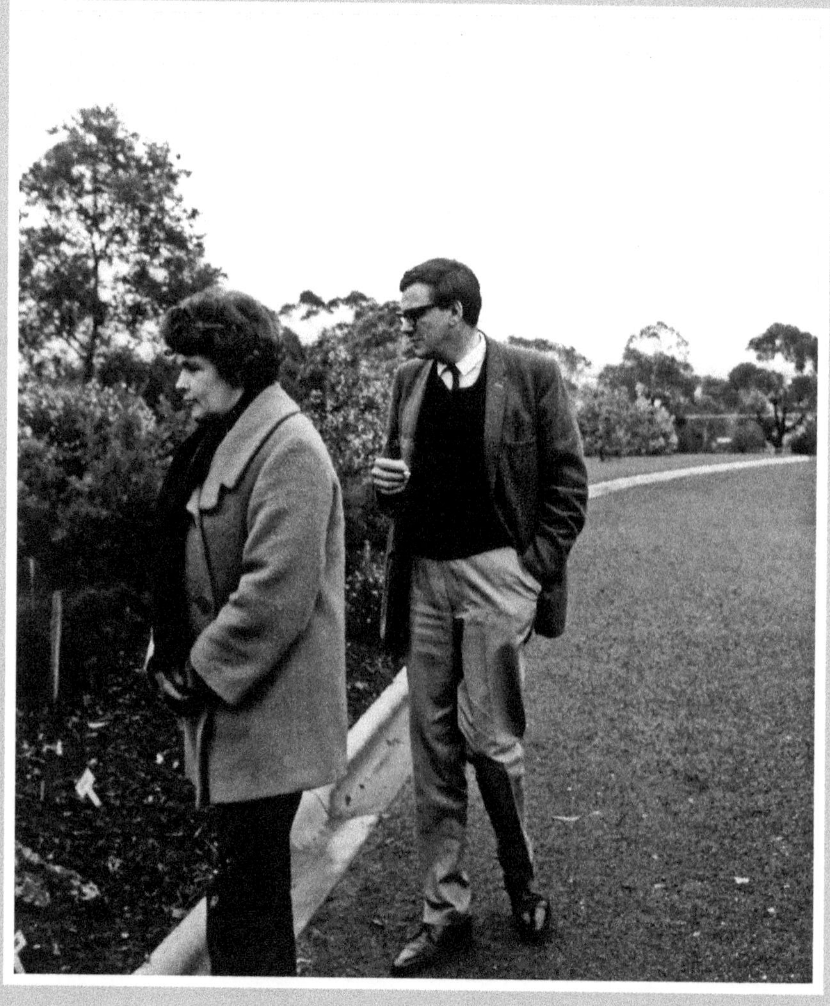

1

Couple in Suburban Civic Garden

In the picture a man and a woman seem to pause on a long path that curves to the right and out of sight. The woman has come fully to a stop, her gloved hands folded against her. She looks towards the left, into a garden bed, perhaps at some plant or shrub that is beyond the border of the black and white image.

He, a few feet behind her, seems to be just coming to a halt. His left foot is off the ground, his toes are just coming down at an angle onto the path. His left knee is bent and his weight is all on his right leg. He too is looking into the garden bed but perhaps not at the same thing that holds the woman's attention.

She has a light smile. The day looks cold. The sky is completely white, perhaps low cloud. The image does not give us any detail in the sky.

He has a cigarette in his right hand. A puff of white smoke stands out against his dark jacket and black jumper. His left hand is in his slacks, the pose is relaxed, casual, despite the white shirt and narrow dark tie.

The image is of a couple taken in the late 1960s or early 1970s. The woman's hair is cut short but full, covering her forehead and shaped so that her cheeks are bare but ears and nape are covered. Her coat is short and double-breasted with big buttons.

They are in a public garden. It is perhaps Sunday afternoon.

Perhaps they are thinking of their own garden and have come to see what looks good and might work at home.

In the ground is a little stick with a square space on which could be written the name of the plant behind it. But our couple are looking beyond this stick, at something out of frame.

It is not clear if they know they are being photographed. There is no one else in the shot. The wide, possibly gravel path is empty, perhaps there are not many people in these public gardens on this cold day.

If the woman's hair and coat suggest the early 1960s the man's attire suggests an earlier time: the short back and sides haircut and black rimmed glasses suggest the 1950s. His jacket is wool and, from the creases in the right sleeve, well-worn. But it is the tie and collar on a Sunday afternoon which really suggests the nineteen-fifties; a dress code that meant when in public, one dressed well and appropriately. It is perhaps the black crewneck jumper that tells us that it is not a working day.

They are dressed well, if conservatively, and they are dressed to be seen in a public place on a weekend day. They are a married couple in their late thirties, early forties.

To tell more about the photograph and people it depicts I will have to go beyond the image, speak of what cannot be seen here. I will not be inferring but telling a story from a fund of stories I could tell about this couple visiting a suburban public garden one weekend day in winter in 1970.

He trained as a doctor then joined a research institute and studied the medical and technological requirements for successful human heart transplants. Then, for a few years, he entered private practice before becoming interested in the mid-sixties in the use of computers in medicine. When the photograph was taken he was the director of a computer study group.

He met his wife at the university. He was interested in the theatre and was a director of the student plays put on at the university in the early 1950s. His wife-to-be had grown up in the outer suburbs of the city and knew few people when she took her place as a student in arts.

Someone suggested that she become involved in a university theatre group. She joined and became a props girl. After they married she left the university without finishing her degree.

In his last year of medicine they had their first child. They went on to have five children in total. Some of these children would be in the public gardens with them. They are somewhere about but not in shot.

I was around fifteen when I took the photograph of my parents.

* * *

I could say that as people my parents were very different, but that would be to say nothing. I could say they had little in common, that I never saw them being close, that their relationship to their children could not have been more dissimilar. That the stance each took as regards the world around them was fundamentally different.

Can I see this in this photograph? My mother is cold and has rugged up with scarf, gloves and overcoat; she stands legs together, the dark of her slacks melding in the black and white photo. Her hands are held close together, perhaps pressed up against the front of her woollen coat. Her thick hair warming the nape of her neck. My mother responds to the world she finds herself in; she keeps herself warm, she is a listener, she hears the world she is a part of.

My father dresses lightly, perhaps he does not feel the cold as much. Perhaps it is not cold at all. His left hand in his pocket may be a concession, maybe just to balance the other hand held comfortably at chest height holding the cigarette not too far away. He is looking into the garden bed, or perhaps not. His lips are pursed, as if something is not quite right; the shrub is not what it claims to be, or is just not in the right place.

It is possible that he is not really paying attention to where he seems to gaze, that he is not even here in these suburban botanical gardens. But the dress is right; he could be anywhere.

❋ ❋ ❋

I thought I might be able to say something about why I chose this picture. I had hoped that my reasons for selecting and writing about this image might be something that belongs to the picture itself.

One reason why I may have chosen this picture is that there are few photos of my parents together. Few images where they share the frame; there are, for instance, no wedding photographs. My mother assured me some years ago that there were a set of pictures taken of the wedding at the church in the hills where my mother had grown up. But she did not have them, she had them once, but they had gone missing.

My father, I know, had a small half-frame 35mm Canon camera. Inserting a roll of 36 frames, he could take 72 pictures on one roll. This is characteristic of my father but I'm not sure why.

He gave me a camera when I was eight years old. It was a Kodak 'brownie box', but it was not a box shape and neither was it brown. A simple spring opened and closed the shutter; the viewfinder was very small and not easy to look through. It took a roll of eight frames using 127 B&W film. The negatives were around 31/2" x 3"; this is a guess, I do not have any of these negatives now.

My father was a scientist, he liked to know how things worked, physics and chemistry and mathematics were the languages that communicated the world to my father.

He showed me how to develop and print these very large negatives using a frame, pressing the newly developed film against a piece of photographic paper clamped together in a metal and glass frame.

I think my father saw himself as a generous man; I think he was genuinely hurt and befuddled when he saw that his gifts of things and knowledge were not, seemingly, what his children wanted from him.

He was not a sharer, after explaining how to process and print the images from my Kodak camera he was not interested in looking at them, nor could they be used to start a conversation; what I thought about my pictures could not be a part of a discussion based on these paper objects. The chemistry yes, the affect no.

I wonder now if my lifelong interest in taking pictures is an unrealised hope that it might be something my father and I might share.

We are a long way from our photograph now, taken on a grey day in winter in a nearly deserted park. But perhaps not, my father did not mind being photographed, perhaps because each photo was not only a piece of science in itself but, that with each click of the shutter, an experiment was being performed, the results never certain, the variables always difficult to control.

My mother did not like being photographed; for her the snatching of a second had something arbitrary about it; why not leave the second as a part of a minute, as a necessary ingredient of an hour, of a day, a lifetime? Taken by the camera, this moment was no longer something being shared, it was something apart.

My mother recently said to me: 'I did not have a watch until I was in my fifties. I never used a camera until I was in my eighties. There were other things that were more important.'

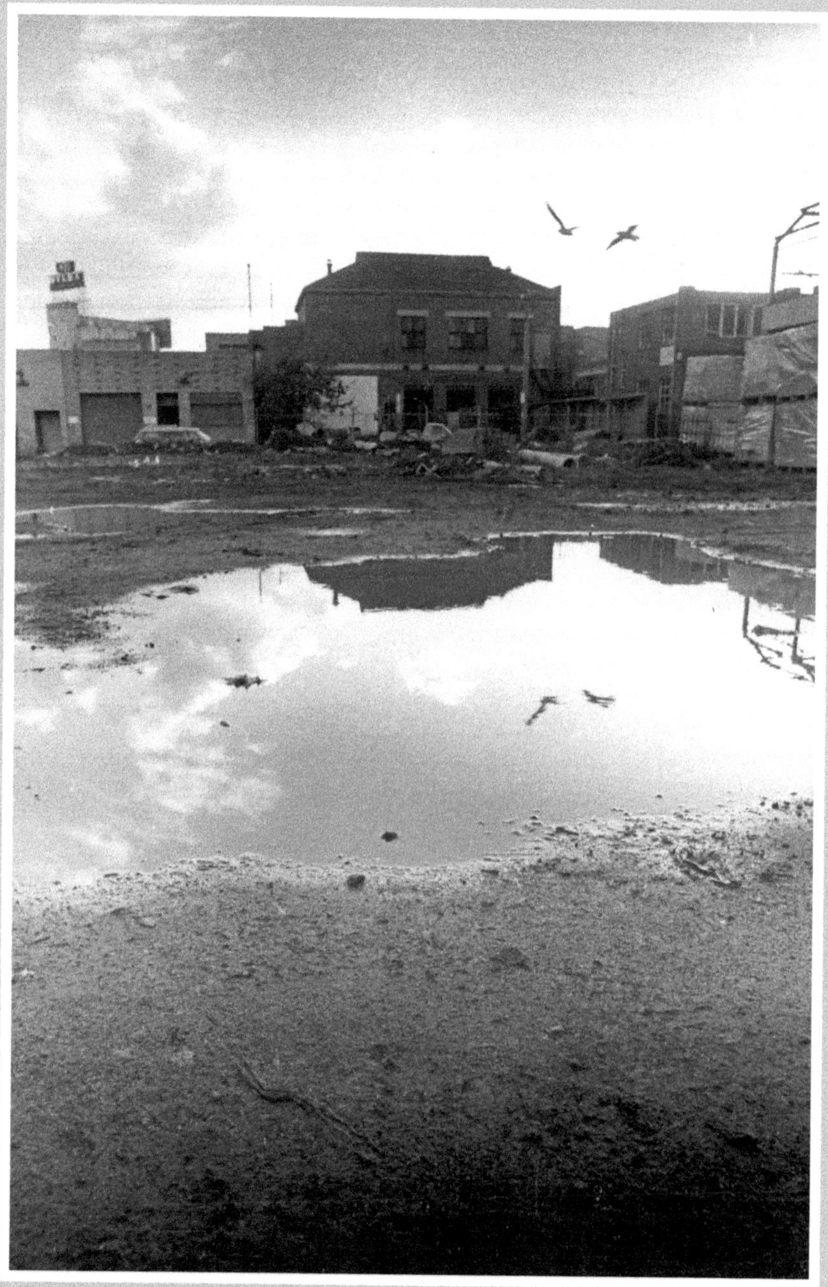

2

Vacant Block

I've always thought of this picture as a picture of emptiness. It is a beautiful photograph and never fails to evoke in me an unquenchable feeling of melancholy. Of course there are many things in this photograph that evince an emptying out; the objects, shapes – all stand for what is not there.

There are no people in this image. Whoever views the photograph is the only person, is the only sentient creature who is able to see the pool of water in the empty block, the two seagulls wheeling low, and the grey silos in the background. And I am outside the scene, beyond the frame looking in from somewhere else.

Within the frame there are no figures, no faces, no animal life, except that of the two birds flying together, close to the ground.

In a way one might say the photo is about the two wide-winged seagulls flying so close together. That this picture is of two seagulls in flight. But I don't think that this is it at all. At best they may be elements setting off the awful absences embodied by this picture.

In the foreground lies an expanse of wet sand. There is nothing on this damp ground except a thin mark, a furrow in the sand made by an animal or bird no longer to be seen.

Within this flat expanse a large pool of water has formed in a patch of ground at a slightly lower level than the surrounding sand. This pool of rainwater takes us into the background where lies a pile of wood and dirt. We can see the grey curves of drainage pipes. On the right at the edge are pallets stacked two high, their unknown contents wrapped in plastic.

Further on we face a wall blocking out half the sky, as if ensuring we are not able to leave the scene of our melancholy. Factories with shuttered driveways, black windows, plain brickwork all give nothing away. It is when looking for a way out that I notice a few cars parked in what must be a narrow street between the empty lot and the factory facades. The vehicles are seen through a wire fence: a station wagon and a ute.

The beauty of this photograph has something to do with its structure. Its hollowness is well constructed. The foreground, middle, and background come in three equal parts, leading the eye by equal movements from the featureless sandy soil at the front, through the pool of water which reflects the sky, up to the dark looming shape of the industrial buildings. There are two other formal aspects I want to mention, firstly, on both left and right edges there are shapes that mirror one another, the Nylex clock atop the concrete silos and opposite, the frame of a new building tapering at the point where the roof is to be placed.

The topography of this image is tightly enclosed. One could say this is a photograph about waiting, everything that is to happen is indicated in absence: the large building site with its pools of water, the tightly wrapped building materials, the skeletal roof frame, the concrete pipes that may be used to drain future downpours.

But to come back to the image's formal qualities that bind us, the elements of a pending future, all caught together in a sense of despair. The main element is the reflection in the pool of water that empties out the centre of the image.

Everything in front of us on the other side of the still water is doubled. And the line of reflection is the doleful black-windowed street with its stationary cars. This line of reflection creates the one-third two-thirds proportions of the classical composition known as the golden ratio, or golden section.

I think this is partly why I find the image both hard to look at and, once immersed, hard to look away from. There is no way out of the structure. The dark high-walled factory in the centre creates a symmetry about the vertical axis and, combined with the horizontal reflection, the image has a double symmetry denying the eye an exit, and the heart any ease.

It is a picture of a cleared building site in Richmond taken by a student of photography, and given to me as a gift. It is possible the street with the parked cars is the street where I lived at the time the photograph was taken in 1979.

My friend's picture is hanging on my wall, clipped tight between glass and chipboard.

I look back at the seagulls: they form a focus in the bilateral symmetry and at the same time create their own mini-symmetry, so closely aligned are they – wings outstretched, bodies tilting. I think it is because the birds are mirrored in the water that they hollow out the image. Become, as it were, signs that there is nothing here: no buildings, no ground, a vacant sky, no warmth to be had from the curiously detailed but blank faces of the buildings we cannot escape gazing at. The birds, despite being together, are so alone in this scene that in identifying with them we empty ourselves out. There is no help for me here: to look is to be caught forever within some terrible vacancy.

And the picture gives the precise moment of our capture, it is 4.36 in the afternoon. The Nylex clock has the numbers in lights. No, we could not be anywhere and, if we know the place, then we know the time. There is something unbearable about all this. There is no room for the dream or reverie here. And yet the clock can suggest a way out – having the precise moment can also mean that another moment, no less precise, that the clock can reveal and, in this way, we can escape: despite the controlling form and structure of the photograph, transience can be ours.

4.36 pm – the only suggestion that anyone can escape this overdetermined moment of sadness. That time can, and will, pass just enough to free us and the formally frozen picture elements from their fixed apprehension.

And yet, even after the digital clock has 'ticked' over and we belong to a moment later, it is the two birds that haunt us. Playful, yet frozen, alive, but only to tell us what is *not here* – twinned, doubled, caught in a subtle geometry that frames all of us at least once.

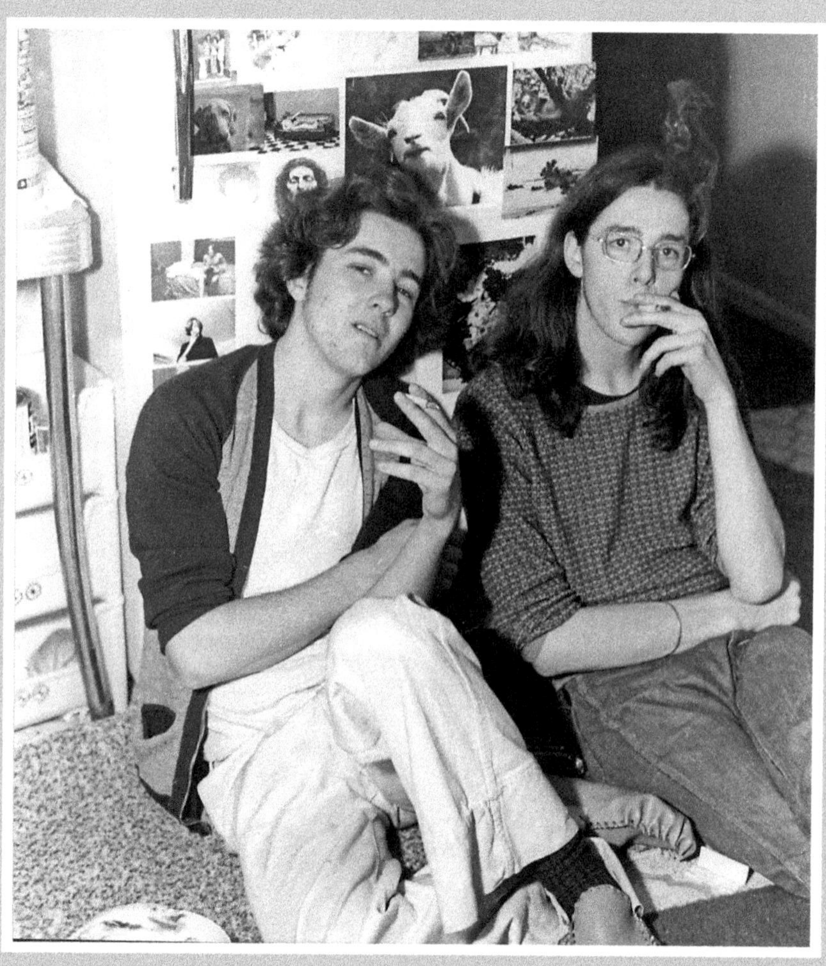

3

Two Young Men Smoking

This is a picture of my friend Ross and I taken in a house we were renting in the winter of 1975 on one of Sydney's northern beaches. We were at the end of our teens.

We are sitting with our backs to the fridge in the kitchen. I do not know who took the photograph. A New Zealand couple had the basement flat, their names I forget, but one of them could have taken the photograph.

We had come to Sydney so Ross could take up a place at the newly opened National Film and Television School. I had applied but had not been successful. I was happy to go to Sydney as I was going to concentrate on my writing rather than pursue film making.

We both grew up in Melbourne. I cannot remember where or exactly when we met but it was certainly photography that brought us together. We were at the same school briefly and the school boasted a darkroom. Perhaps we met there? Neither of us liked the school we were attending. At the end of year eleven while his parents were away on holiday Ross left and went to an experimental school which offered photography as a year 12 subject.

I remember making a small animated film with Ross. A hand-wound Bolex camera loaded with 16mm black and white film was secured to a tripod and pointed down to the floor where hand-drawn pictures were laid out. Ross had drawn a skyscape in coloured pencils on a big sheet of paper. On smaller pieces of paper we had drawn and cut out clouds, an airliner, skyscrapers and hills dotted with farm animals. We arranged our movable cut-out pictures and Ross would fire off a few frames. Then we would move the airliner and clouds and landscape and again take a few frames.

We were both engrossed in making this short cartoon. Using the viewfinder on the Bolex we ensured the background paper filled the whole frame. We made sure the paper was weighted to the linoleum of the vestibule floor and would not move as we arranged frame by frame the 'moving' image we were filming. A lot of work was in shifting our aeroplane across the many-pieced sky just enough to ensure a smooth flight as the movie unfolded.

The animation was called *Falling* and lasted only a few minutes. Our jetliner flew over landscapes, a city, the countryside, it flew through clouds and towards the end a figure fell from the plane, fell through the empty sky to the ground. Ross put a soundtrack to the little film, Peggy Lee singing 'Is That All There Is?'

For me it was a great deal. I had learnt some real magic. Ross had shown me how things were put together; how animation worked. We saw a lot of movies together. Fellini, Wertmuller, Pasolini, Werner Herzog, and Visconti were all still making films: the work of these filmmakers configured how, as 16 year-olds, we could see the world, could learn a way of understanding what was all around us.

So here we are, a few years later, sitting on the kitchen floor having our photograph taken. Behind us covering the fridge door are more photographs. A goat looks over our heads, perhaps alert to the lion reclining on a tree branch. On the left is another reclining figure, Ross's brother on a couch, then another animal, a Weimaraner dog, one of two who lived downstairs with the New Zealanders.

A Japanese print on a postcard. A photograph of a pencil drawing of a head and, above Ross's right shoulder, two snaps of me taken years before.

I sit now, in front of *this* collection of photographs, and wonder why it is this image I have chosen from so many. Just as I ask what led to the collection of these particular images on the fridge door that we selected? Perhaps there is just one rule that governs both selections? That at any given time there is just one collection to be displayed.

It is like asking what made us such good friends; good at being with one another and perhaps even good at friendship itself? Looking at this photograph now some forty-five years later I am struck by the similarity of our poses against the crowded fridge door: the placement of our arms even to the positions of our hands holding the rolled cigarettes. The unengaged fingers relaxing away from the index and third fingers. Our heads tilt in the same direction. Our handedness is different: so why does Ross smoke with his left hand? Is some sort of unconscious symmetry perhaps suggested here?

We can't see my footwear. I have on, perhaps, calf-length Cuban-heeled leather boots. The knitted jumper was given to me for a birthday – 'the Italian special' Ross called it, his tone of voice suggesting he wasn't being purely descriptive. Ross often wore his moccasins which were often matched with the zipped grey towel cardigan and white T-shirt.

At sixteen Ross was a cross-country runner, played the clarinet, and was seldom without an apple to polish and consume. He sang Loving Spoonful songs and, together with his brother, could recite Goon skits in the accents and tonalities of Eccles and Neddy Seagoon.

He was the youngest of three and introduced me to the music of a slightly older cohort, his sister and her circle. Bob Dylan, The

Velvet Underground. His sister's partner was an artist. The head on the fridge is one of his early drawings.

I remember myself as slightly overblown when we met; sometimes silent other times theatrical; I was unhappy and struggled to think, finding panic an all too common response to adolescence. Ross was more measured and reduced my double-time to something more manageable. David Bowie had a big influence on me, his confidence in uncertainty and ambiguity I found reassuring. Not so for Ross; he found something very disturbing in Bowie's image of himself as half-dog, half-man on the cover of *Diamond Dogs*.

At nineteen we shared a half-house. During the day we worked on one another's short 16mm films. Late at night we would drive into Carlton to a pool hall called Johnny's Green Room. A big, quiet pool hall, strips of bright light illuminating the full size tables. After the chaos of the day I think we liked the quiet, the pools of dark shadow, the murmur of voices slipping around the four sides of the busy tables.

We played for hours, quickly, competitively, chalking, squinting, lining up, judging the angles. And then, relinquishing our cigarette, leaning over, our eye along the shiny wood, we would play the shot.

We played game after game, rolled cigarette after cigarette, usually until the blue light of the early morning managed to slide between the wall and the edge of the pulled blinds.

We seldom spoke to anyone else playing and, on only one occasion, were we disturbed in our concentration. One morning some plain clothes police came in and worked one table at a time demanding, when they got to us, that we roll up our sleeves. Looking for track marks, for users.

It was cold in the mornings but we were wide awake, knowing the next thing was just around the corner.

We drove to Sydney in a car my father gave me in return for

me selling my Triumph motorcycle. The car, a Morris 1100, was old and not well looked after, I had no mechanical knowledge preferring my line that for tools 'I carried a 1/4" spanner and a tin of cut and polish in the glove box.'

Somewhere up on the Hume Highway the engine started to splutter, then it stopped and we glided to the edge of the highway. We ended up at a garage where there was no mechanic. Ross proposed we stay overnight by the service station, sleep in our sleeping bags and, in the morning, strip the carburettor.

Even now I can recall my astonishment at this suggestion. Neither of us knew anything about car engines but Ross, unlike me at the time, was able to think things through. The next day we were shown a bench under a tin roof out the back of the garage where we could work.

My barely controlled panic at the broken down car and the enormous distances yet to be travelled kept me silent as Ross found the carburettor under the bonnet. Then, with tools generously loaned by the garage, we carefully took out the part. During that day of quiet concentration, I was given one of the most profound lessons in thinking in my life.

Humming and singing snatches of songs Ross, working from left to right, on a swept and dusted plywood bench top, slowly began to disassemble the part he felt sure was the problem: fuel was not getting into the engine from the tank. The carburettor was dirty and we were going to take it apart and clean it.

One by one, each screw, washer, seal, and manifold was laid out on the bench: the grammar of the device that combined the air and fuel into a ratio that, when sucked into the engine, would combust thus forcing the cylinders into motion. Each moveable piece was laid bare, examined, and cleaned with cloth and oil, then set down in order on the bench.

It was hot, the bench beneath its pitched tin roof stood close to the scrub and forest, the warm wind blew in all directions as we worked out how each piece fitted into the next; clips, spring washers, tiny screws some with Phillips heads. In doing this we came to understand what each piece did in the assembly. Ross was calm and methodical; he did not know the answer, but he knew how to approach the problem.

And when the car started, Ross was pleased but not surprised. It was this lack of surprise that taught me that there could be a discernible logic that could make sensible the seeming inscrutable world around me.

A little later, a matter of months after the photo was taken, we went our separate ways. For the next quarter of a century we met only a few times, and then briefly, and not at all for the last 18 of those years.

That the photograph was taken at a pivotal point we were not aware. Everything that had gone before was not to be reprised and the future would not contain a portrait such as the one here. But the photo cannot show any of this – it cannot, does not, relate that story, or any other story based on the two people depicted. It has perhaps just become an excuse to tell a story, any story, told by anyone prepared to unspool a narrative.

Or perhaps the photo forestalls narrative? Its elements are all on display; there is nothing to unpick here, everything is shown; we know the names for all the things here.

The story is always extraneous, an add-on, told by those who remember the time, the moment, the place but not perhaps the photograph. And for someone who does not know the people and place depicted in the image there is no story possible.

We knew little of one another's life when, much later, we met up accidentally in a cafe. In a way, standing together in the cafe, we were as the two in the photograph: cut off from the past and present, outside a narrative that might connect us to a viewer, to a stream of time passing. In the cafe we knew neither's story of the last twenty-five years. The story of wives and partners, of children, work, health and home was all, at that moment, extrinsic to the frame. We recognised one another, but of our recent lives knew not enough to make any sort of a narrative.

What we did know was that we were still friends – perhaps knowing friendship means you don't have to know much at all, outside the frame everything is just contingency.

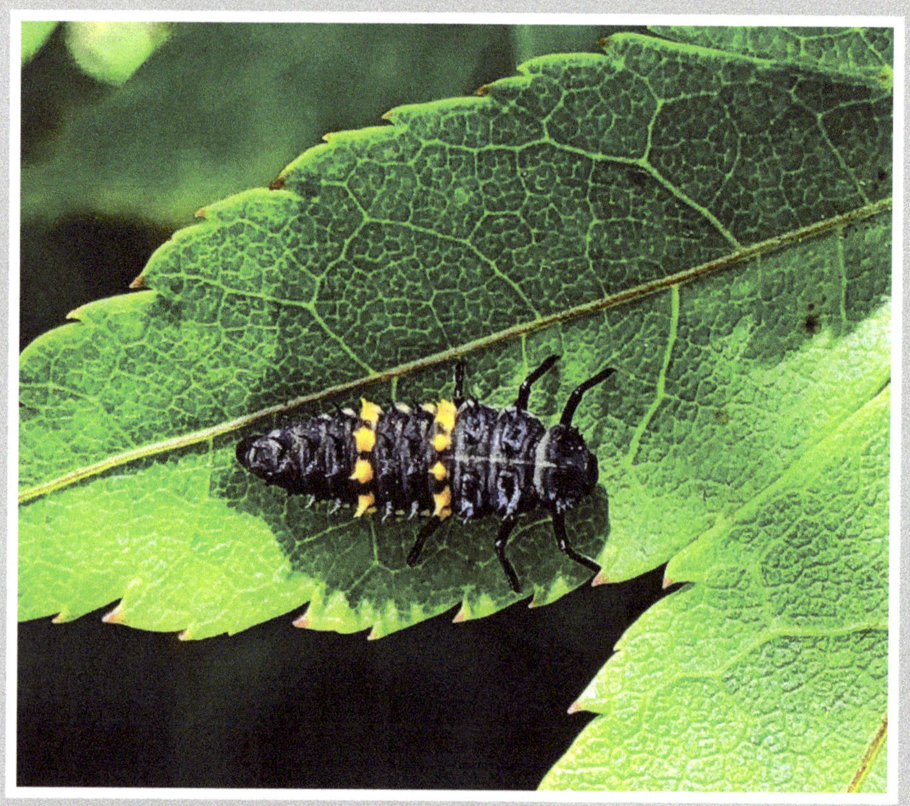

4

Arthropod

I didn't know what this creature was when I spotted it one day in late November. For me, Spring begins with the new growth on the bare limbed Japanese maple. New bright pale red stems appear from the tips of last year's growth. Two new stems fork and once they have grown a centimetre or so they sprout another pair of red forks. It is from these shoots that the leaves will bud and open. When they appear, they resemble a human palm with the fingers pressed together. They unfold stickily from the pupa-like casing that peels back uncovering the folded leaf inside. The palmate leaf opens, seven lobes spreading apart. The surface of the leaves I see are partially covered with a bright white filament. I have no idea what this is but it soon disappears as the leaf holds itself open to the sun.

I am used to coming out in the mornings to examine whatever I might find on the *Acer palmatum* which grows by the path out to the back yard. For some reason this particular specimen attracts a multitude of insects and arachnids in Spring. This is in contrast to another specimen planted at the same time and now roughly the same size but which grows on the north side of the house and carries no burden of arthropods.

The creature in the photograph was one of the creatures I discovered on the east-facing *Acer*. In the photograph the creature is enlarged some 13 times, the detail of the surface of the leaf on which it sits gives some sense of scale. The animal is just 10–12mm long and 2mm at its widest.

It sits on one of the serrated lobes of the leaf, on the edge, and near the gap between the adjoining lobes. When I first saw it I thought it was a rather basic creature, every aspect seemed blocked in, not finished; a rough try for a real animal. It does not have the three part structure of an insect: head, thorax, abdomen, not even the two parts of a typical arachnid.

It displays a basic bilateral symmetry with clearly etched segments going down either side. It sports legs that seem as organic as Allen keys, matt black, and bent so the ends touch the surface and hold the animal upright. The creature's eyes to be guessed at by the change of tones in shiny black patches and a mouth suggested at by the barely tapered front.

But what struck me was the yellow bands. These, when seen close, as in the photograph, are not continuous bands of colour but are yellow raised patches on the animal's back that thin to a spike. When I focus on these pyramidal structures I see that all the segments of the creature carry these spikes. As in keeping with the rough and ready structure, these spikes seem to be attached to the surface rather than be growing organically out of the carapace. The black spikes look like the rough-cut nails called blue cut tacks.

The coloured bands at segments three and six create a distinct black and yellow pattern. I knew that black and yellow in the animal world is a warning to stay away. It warns prey that the bearer of such colouration is toxic. I look up this warning sign and see that this is known as aposematic colouring and is used by insects, reptiles and some mammals. The word comes from the Greek for 'sign' and 'away'. Nothing could be clearer.

I watch the creature roam about on the green leaf. When I see it bend into a crescent shape as it turns I like it even less. I wonder what it is that it eats.

I see that all the new growth on the *Acer* is infested with aphids. These pale, seemingly featureless insects swarmed over the pale sticky lobes of the new leaves. These insects are sucking the new sugars forming in the delicate stems and leaves as they began to photosynthesise in the warm days.

The aphids can be several layers deep on the new thin red stems. They obscure the new growth completely with their grey and pink bodies so that the stems more resembled stick insects moving in most unnatural ways.

About the same time of this infestation I noticed labybird beetles appearing on the leaves and stems of the Spring growth. I thought they must be preying on the aphids.

I was able to identify the species of ladybird beetle by counting the spots and matching the number and the colouration to images of the common spotted ladybird beetle *Harmonia conformis* (23 black spots on the red wing covers).

Some days I go out to inspect the tree and I see lines of small ants marching up the trunks of the *Acer* and into the canopy. Once out on the sunny surfaces of the leaves they pause and wave their antennae. I have heard of ants 'farming' aphids, harvesting beads of excreted sugar. But I don't see this.

The thick new foliage creates layers of leaves allowing insects to shelter from the sun while moving about. I distinguished several species of ants and flies that all come to the maple and stay. There are several species of small spider living on the tree. I saw a small black spider eating a winged insect, the black veined transparent wings were all that could be seen as the arachnid stiffly ate its meal.

I am guessing that this spider is a species of jumping spider of which there are an uncounted and unnamed number in this country. I have managed to photograph several that live and hunt amongst the leaves of the *Acer*. One spider, festooned with white filaments, I have tentatively identified as *Opisthoncus mordax*. Hairy-legged with a black shiny chitinous carapace, this spider appeared from between two leaves that were bound together with silver webbing. Strands still trail from the spiders spinnerets as he moves towards me on the leaf. Carcasses, wound in white, lie on the green surface where the jumping spider comes to a stop, its black shiny eyes catch the sunlight as I move back.

However my favourite is a very small jumping spider that I struggled to bring into focus using my phone camera. Like *O. mordax*, this pinkish hairy spider used two leaves as a floor and ceiling, binding them together with spun walls of white thread. This creature seldom comes out of its shelter, just its head protrudes from under the bright green leaf.

This creature takes my attention because of the markings on its head, in certain light it appears that there is a grinning face looking back up at me. Two large black spots outlined by white lines suggest a joined eyebrow and the line of a 'nose' running down between the two 'eyes' suggested by the black spots.

Below is a wide black band edged in hairs suggesting teeth in a black mouth. I have looked for this creature in lists of jumping spiders but have found no description or image resembling what I see when I look into the bound leaves of the *Acer*. Do my eyes miss-see, or do I invent my photographs, conjuring imaginary animals from my out-of-focus pixels?

The other specimen of the *Acer* planted at the same time is completely free from this chain of being. The southern specimen may not be as healthy as the northern specimen. It may be weakened by the conditions of its existence. It is partly shaded by a large golden elm. The maple is surrounded by clumps of flag iris and day lilies. Maybe this is enough to make it prey to aphids which then bring other arthropods to the tree.

But it survives the aphids and the lack of afternoon sun, and it flowers and forms seed and grows new branches. Admittedly, these somewhat spindly branches attempt to reach out from under the elm whose branches and leaves radiate through an arc of 150° and tower above the *Acer*.

The creature in my photograph enlarged to monstrous dimensions is not anything of its own. It is a transient form and appears, as it does here, for only a few days before shedding its outer form and appearing as something slightly different again. It is a larval creature, eating whatever it can find, aphids, its own siblings and even eggs such as the ones from which it has recently hatched. Larva is a word from the Latin meaning a spectre, a ghost, something present, perceptible but not real, not of this world. This larva will grow so fat that its covering, its constraining cuticle, will crack open and a new creature will emerge to continue to forage and then, in its turn, moult and become something else once again.

This is an image of an instar, a stage in the larva's metamorphosis into a thing in itself. At each splitting of the exoskeleton this creature will emerge with a slightly different shape. Once I saw an instar with only one band of yellow spikes around its 6th segment. Instar, another Latin word, means form, figure, or likeness, perhaps chosen to acknowledge the transient nature of the creature. It bears no likeness to the adult or imago which is why it took me sometime to realise it was a passing form in the life cycle of the ladybird beetle, *Harmonia conformis*.

I suppose I did not consider it a larval stage of the ladybird, beetle because, watching the green leaves of the *Acer*, I saw both creatures, the elongated, yellow-banded bendy thing and the hemispherical shiny black spotted beetle that, occasionally, would burst into wing and disappear in an instant.

But this creature has hatched from an egg deposited by the adult beetle under the maple leaves and is now undergoing a process that leads to it forming a pupa. So the larva grows; not quite anything of its own but four stages of something which it won't resemble in the slightest. I have seen adult ladybird beetles crawling on the same leaf as their larva: one globular, its parts hidden under glossy hard wing casings, the other lugubrious, clipped together roughly, its elongated form bristling with yellow and black spikes.

This photo is an image of one of the four mysterious instars this creature must pass through before it forms a pupa and then, within this sheath, it will be biochemically broken down and reformed into the adult imago – the very image of the thing.

We are in a welter of forms, images, likenesses, ghosts, figures as we try to pin this creature down, hold it from transience, make it something in itself. But we must wait out the continual change and shape shifting that comprise the metamorphosis of this beetle.

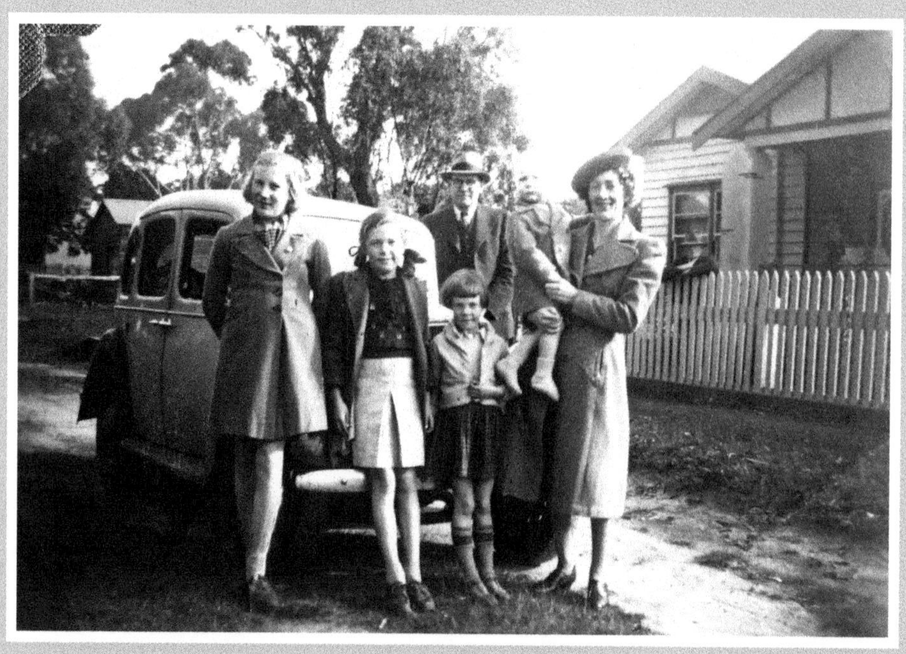

5

A Family Outing

It is strange to say that family photo albums were made with little thought as to identifying the images they held. Traditional albums, physical books, were usually comprised of blank black pages interleaved with semi-transparent tissue paper. The pages of these books were wider than they were high. These pages were often held in place with a woollen cord that ran through the front and back covers.

Everything about this design made labelling the photos quite difficult. The black page couldn't be written on with pen or biro, the textured surface did not hold the ink and, of course, without contrast between page and dark ink the words could not be read. Finally, the photograph themselves were printed on a shiny paper which did not absorb ink.

Sometimes things were written on the back of a photo; presumably this is why they were affixed to the page with the application of glued corners into which you fitted the right-angled corners of the rectangular photos. But, from the front, there was no way to *tell* if there was information written on the back of the image.

So, usually, images were pasted onto the black landscape format page with no information as to who, when, or where. Of course we know it's Frank and Stella down on the foreshore last summer when they first got engaged, Brett took the picture on his Kodak.

All this is vivid, and those to whom you were showing the photo all nodded, knowing that Frank was a bit of a chancer and Stella would be with child soon. We know the beach because we often went there as a family, and who could forget the wedding a few months later when it rained? No-one of course.

Then one day no-one remembers any of it. None of the people who were a part of that narrative are still alive. A postcard sitting in a rack in the local newsagents has more information, tells a greater story than any of the photos in this old family album.

Perhaps it is our unspoken understanding that soon, not now, but later on, these people, this place, ourselves will be history, not something personal but something indifferent, just a part of some sweep of time that will remove all this, as we use our broom to collect up all the dust settling in the brightly lit hallway.

So what care should we have for names and dates, places and people? This beach scene mounted in its four cut corners on the page, with all of us now gathered around, adding our bit to the story of the engaged couple frolicking in the shallows of a suburban beach?

So to, this photo of a group, a family group, posed rather carefully in front of a car. I came across it in an album lent to my mother by her brother. As with all family photos, I know these people but I don't – the newly seen image seems to cast doubt on any of my so-called knowings. Whenever I come to look at this photo, I have to start again. I have to look carefully to recognise these people if I can.

It is not the strange pose, the quaint costumes, the setting, it is that these people inhabit a world that I do not, could never have been a part of, yet they are completely necessary to my ever having any world to inhabit.

Recently I spent an afternoon with someone whom I did not

recognise. We had apparently met among common friends some 50 years ago. When she got out of her car, this woman said 'oh I remember you well', smiling at me. That day we spent time in our host's garden, harvesting tomatoes, beans, and plucking sweet corn from tall plants. It was a strange feeling, she remembered me; but, for me it was as if we never had met.

Something of that feeling comes over me when I look at this photo of this well-dressed prosperous-looking family. They are all dressed for the occasion (whatever that may be). My aunt on the left in a buttoned wool coat with a cravat neatly tied about her throat looks at the photographer with a slightly suspicious look; her tilted head and gaze not without threat. With her hands behind her back and legs crossed, she seems to be avoiding the photographer, making herself the smallest target possible in her otherwise exposed situation.

My mother beside her looks directly at the camera, her hands relaxed by her sides. Two years younger than her sister, she has hair in two pigtails tied in ribbons and wears a neat pleated skirt. Standing behind her and the car is my grandfather looking straight at the camera – he had no fear of the device. In his younger days he was a photographer of the bush. He used glass plates to record his images of uncut mountain ash and vast lakes in the wilderness.

The youngest of the four children is my uncle whose album this image is from; he is being held in his mother's arms. My uncle is about two in this picture and, like the others around the car, is dressed in a warm woollen coat. Their formal attire puzzles me, perhaps they have driven out to visit someone, or perhaps they are dressed in best clothes for the unknown photographer? If so, this becomes a formal photo taken by a professional photographer. Was there an occasion? A birthday, an anniversary, had the car just been purchased? The picture is properly lit, well exposed, and there has been thought given to the composition and the placement of all the participants: they are all front on, no person is obscuring anyone else. The roadway and position of the car create an diagonal which draws the eye into the image.

But who is the little girl with the short cropped hair staring intently at the picture taker? Her hand pulls at the edges of her jacket, it ill-fits her. Her short plaid skirt and long banded socks suggest a school uniform, perhaps the jacket is an afterthought? Something to give her a more formal look and to cover up her school shirt?

The ten-year-old girl standing next to her, my mother, now in her eighties has no idea of who the little girl beside her is. Perhaps even at the time, guessed at 1941, she did not know who the little girl was who came to stand in this rather formal family portrait.

And then there is the man in the background, he leans on a picket fence his arms crossed over the white painted points. Behind him is a well kept weatherboard house. What strikes me is that his gaze is directed at the photographer, ignoring the family group around the car. The brim of his hat is pulled low over his forehead and his thin lips are parted as he gazes intently.

He, too, like us, is curious about why this moment might serve as an occasion for a professional photograph: the tripod, the bellows lens, a black cape draped over the photographer as he composes his image of a family all smiling at the camera.

It is only mother and her brother who are still alive from this family group and neither can say who the little girl is nor the intent watcher over the fence.

The viewer here, in this room almost eighty years later, is smiling at the elegant young woman who would become his grandmother, the two-tone hat at an angle allowing her curly hair to cascade down one side of her face. Her beautiful fitted long coat, her smile as she balances her youngest child on her hip. And the little girl who will be my mother is looking at me with a smile I know so well.

Postscript

My mother, who no longer drives, asked me to take her down to visit her brother who had just turned eighty. We drove down to a small town on the coast where my uncle and his wife have just moved to last year. My mother was going to stay with them for a few days.

Over lunch we talked of family and I showed my uncle the picture of him as a child with his family standing against the Ford Prefect. He and my mother, who had not been able to tell me much about the image, slowly began to piece together a story about this photo.

Like putting together a jigsaw puzzle, they picked over bits of information, fragments they then studied, turned this way and that in an attempt to fit them together to make a coherent narrative encompassing the image before them.

My mother and her brother guessed, second guessed and, over the next hour or so, came up with this story; extended the single moment of the photograph over many years, involving many places and people.

It was a picture of my mother's father's family at Glenthompson in the Western District, at the home of their father's sister. The family had come up all the way from where they lived in the Dandenong Ranges to visit in the school holidays. There was some discussion of possible names and my mother and her brother finally settled on Amy as the name of their father's sister.

Neither sibling remembered the particular day the photo was taken or why they were all dressed up.

I asked about the man leaning on the fence, and my uncle asked his sister: 'Is that Amy's husband. What was his name?' My mother shook her head, 'A butcher perhaps?'. 'Les, his name was, Les. A dour man', my uncle nodded satisfied with his recall. 'He was a slaughterman.' 'Yes', said my mother. 'I remember the single row of roses planted on the path to the house, I remember thinking that they were mean.'

As for the little girl. They thought she must be their cousin, Amy's daughter. But only because she was there in the photo; neither my mother nor her brother remembered *her*, nor did they have a name to give her.

My mother enjoyed her stay with her brother and his wife. They went on day trips to interesting spots in the area. Later my uncle told me he enjoyed 'having big sis around for a few days'.

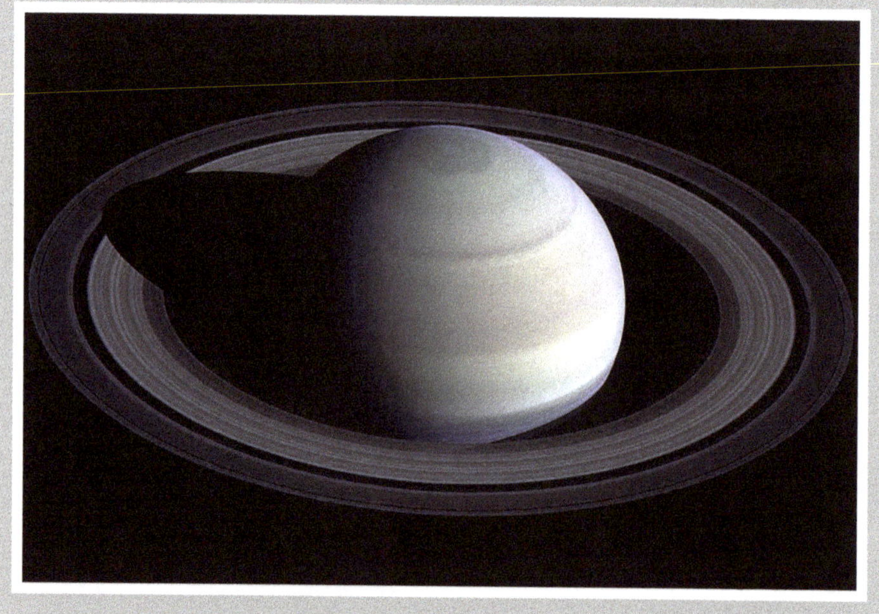

6

Saturn by Cassini

This image is rather difficult to talk about. It is a picture of an object inconceivably far away, it is also inconceivably large. We have the numbers, we have the distances, we even have names. But still this image is almost impossible to talk about.

Once I had it pinned to a cork board on the doorway of the workroom. Every time I passed the door I had to look and, when I did, everything else stopped; what I was doing what I was thinking. I had to take it down. It fills my heart like water in a reservoir.

I dimly understand that, when I look at this picture, I am looking at a picture of Saturn but am experiencing something else. That perhaps is something I cannot talk about: something that is not conceivable.

So that leaves me with the words I can use to identify the image. It is a photograph taken with a wide angled camera from the Cassini spacecraft of the northern hemisphere of Saturn in April 2016. The Sun, some 1.437 million kilometres away, provides the light that reflects off the surface of the planet and its rings into Cassini's wide angle lens.

It took Cassini seven years to come out from Earth to orbit Saturn. Seven years in silence, flying in a near vacuum through black space. Seven years unseen and unthought of by most everyone except those given responsibility for its mission out among the gas giants of the Solar System. In a way you could say this image is a picture of silence.

There is something uncanny about the light that illuminates the planet and that throws such a sharp and discrete shadow, the shadow of an enormous sphere that falls across the fine grained rings that encircle the pale planet.

This light falling so far away is also the light that casts shadows on the leaves of an espalier climbing rose outside my window.

But what does the light reaching Saturn illuminate? It shows us something not quite imaginable; a picture of what I cannot imagine.

* * *

This image was taken when the northern hemisphere of Saturn was approaching the Summer Solstice. This was the longest day in a Summer that lasts for 7½ Earth years. The grey green planet is surrounded by its rings. The rings seem to cradle the planet. Its sharp summer shadow creates a tight black arc across the myriad rings that encircle the cloud-bound planet.

Looking through Cassini's camera I see the outer layers of ammonia ice from a distance of three million kilometres. The planet is given shape by the faint banding across its surface, bulging at the equator and flattened at the poles.

Around the northern pole there whirls a hexagonal shaped jet stream.

The planet is all exteriors – layers of ammonia ice, water ice, ammonium hydrosulphide, metallic hydrogen. But beneath these ever denser layers there is no surface, the descent is forever.

No-one can land here; I can never come here. Once caught in the planet's orbit I am like Cassini, not even human despite my array of sensory apparatus, but transfixed knowing I can only look and yet perhaps not understand a thing of what I am seeing.

Even the Huygens lander brought all the way out here to the

edge of the Solar System was only to land on Titan, Saturn's largest moon. A moon with a climate that creates an Earth-like surface of rivers, lakes, dunes, and which is seasonal with a methane cycle analogous to that of Earth's hydrologic cycle.

This is a long way away; when I look at this image I feel a long way away. When I look at this picture the wind is knocked out of me, I am disembodied; it is all a little too much. The continuous surface glows; the rings circle in infinite detail.

I wonder once again what I am seeing: it may not be this picture, it may not be Saturn, but another picture of a planet in space. A bubblegum card, that's what I have in front of me. The confection is unwrapped and the shiny greaseproof paper crackles faintly as I hold the coloured cardboard square that has my complete attention.

The time and place has gone, I am alone in an empty room perhaps 8 or 9 years old. I don't think about anything. And whatever has my attention is embodied in the coloured drawing of the pale planet at the centre of its infinite circling coloured rings.

* * *

I am sometimes aware that not everyone is interested in pictures of other worlds. The grey-orange rocky landscapes of Mars, whole valleys and hills, dust and water coursed plains.

Perhaps I should not be surprised that people cannot see what I see. For I do not know what I see. I experience the effects but not the understanding: faulty telemetry perhaps, but if everything is something other, then no recording or transmission can ever convey what is seen or felt. I read in pages from the Jet Propulsion Laboratory that the telemetry from Cassini's wide angle camera show us Saturn's colours as we would see them if we were there looking with our own eyes.

Awe, beauty, etc., perhaps come before everything else, the substance, the light and dark are titrated out later. And here am I with these words perhaps just transmuting gold into lead. The alchemists knew to speak was to fail in the great enterprise.

It was late at night and I was on my own watching television. There was a program on the Cassini-Huygens mission. How could I not watch it way past my bedtime? Suddenly I felt tears popping into the corners of my eyes. I sat up: on the screen was something I'd not imagined before in my views of this distant planet. We were now on the other side of the planet, the Sun's direct light was blocked out, and below a silhouetted Saturn, beyond the strangely lit rings was a blue point, and they were telling me this was Earth.

I was suddenly there, and yet I was looking back to where I could only be – all at the same time. In either place I was still an incomprehensible long way away, looking at something that was inconceivable.

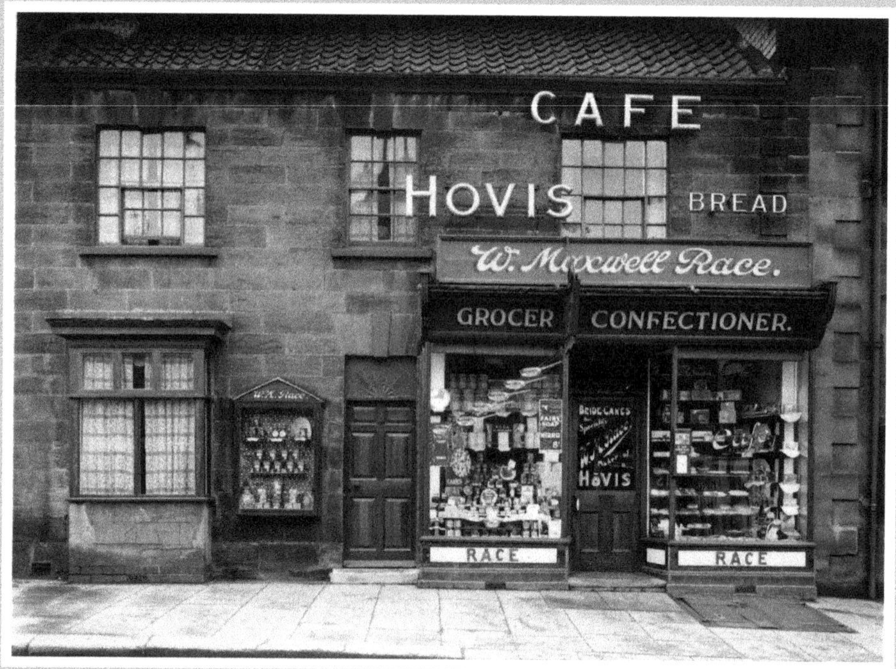

CAFE
HOVIS
BREAD
W. Maxwell Race.
GROCER
CONFECTIONER.
BRIDE CAKES
HOVIS
RACE
RACE

7

Yorkshire Shopfront

This is a picture of the shopfront of my great-grandfather's business in Loftus, Yorkshire. W Maxwell Race was a baker, confectioner and grocer. Upstairs, and in rooms to the side, he and his wife, Sarah, brought up eight children, two boys and six girls. Their second son, Ernest, was my grandfather.

Three generations of the Race family worked and lived behind this shopfront. Robert came from inland Aycliffe and set up business in the 1860s on the south side of Market Place. The market place was an area on either side of High St large enough for traders to set up stalls on market day, local fairs were also held here.

The address for Robert Maxwell's shop was 81-83 High St. His son W Maxwell was born in 1851 and it is his name that adorns the shopfront in the picture. Maxwell was Robert's wife's maiden name, and W Maxwell took over the business on the death of his father in 1891.

Behind the somewhat forbidding exterior were confected a wide range of cakes, pastries, biscuits and breads. W Maxwell baked bread using the flour milled by Hovis Co. Ltd who had recently set up in Cheshire. Signage boasts that ornate cakes for weddings, bride cakes, were a specialty of the baker. In the right display window you can just see fresh pies and cakes set out.

Groceries could also be bought and, though it is difficult to see into the dim interior, I can just make out labelled jars and the name Carr's, who still makes crackers.

A printed advertisement for W Maxwell Race, written in the same font as that of the shop front signage says that he was awarded 'Two Silver Medals for Pastries Etc.' Cream goods are also said to be a specialty, so the ad suggests 'Give Us a Trial Order'.

I suppose what strikes me about the picture is all the stone: stone walls, stone pavement, broken only by the windows and even these are segmented into small panes like the pattern of brickwork.

The roof tiles with thin grey and black edges move with stiff regularity over the sloping roof, echoing the pattern of the wall and ground beneath them.

There is no greenery in the picture of any sort, no grass, no window boxes, no cut flowers in vases, let alone any suggestion of trees or bushes.

I am going to look beyond the frame of this picture and, to do this, I am going to imagine my great-grandfather W Maxwell coming through the shop out the front door and into the street. I am going to have my imagined W Maxwell describe the street. He is taking a break after an early morning baking the day's bread. The loaves are coming out of the oven. I place him on a sunny morning a few years before his death at seventy-two in 1923.

W Maxwell bustles through the shop taking off his apron, opening the door and going into the street. He looks back, scanning the displays in the windows to see if all is as it should be.

Across the high street opposite was J.M. Slater, the pharmacist. They had been there forever, though they had diversified, adding to pills and powder, cameras and film. Now they called themselves chemists and opticians; the son was now a member of the Institute of Opticians. I suppose that makes him the right person to sell photographic equipment.

He knew the advertisement for the new Kodak cameras: 'Fold them up and carry them in your pocket'. Very modern. A long way from glass plates. He briefly considered going over, but there was nothing wrong with his eyes. He lifted his round face to the warming sun.

Not wishing to go back in, W Maxwell looked past the Slaters' place towards the Post Office next door and next, dwarfing that modest shop, the three storey National Provincial and Liverpool Bank. He narrowed his eyes, perhaps it was the bright morning light but maybe it was to look at the pointed Gothic arches of the bank's shallow portico: as a good Wesleyan the arches and pillars had a bit too much of Rome about them for his liking.

Which, in turn, reminded him that it was choir practice tonight and he would be conducting in front of a small audience in the Newham Chapel. Plenty to do before then and, leaning out a little, he read the time on the Town Hall clock above the old wool store down to his left. Turning back to the market place, he caught sight of someone out on the Angel Inn balcony, probably cleaning as the sun wasn't high enough even to warm the glass enclosure.

He better get down and help Max, his eldest son, load up the delivery van which now took bread, cakes and groceries all about. It was all Max's idea, and he had been pretty much running things for the last few years: not only could they stock the Zetland Rd premises but the van could travel for many miles around and never get tired or want oats. But he wasn't going to drive it! Leave it to Max and his apprentice.

W Maxwell slapped at his thighs, flour flew off brightly and he turned left past the stone portico outside the Golden Lion next door. He nodded his greetings to the hotel regulars before turning into Lingberry Garth which was, apart from the ironmongers on the corner, really just the rear access for both the pub and the bakery yard. Lawrence's boys were out front as usual putting out the stands of goods: coils of wire, spades, hoes and the like. But the way was wide enough to display balers, carders, threshers and grass cutters for the farmers around Loftus. All the stuff he would see out front of his place on the days when the wool fair would stage a parade.

Still, he hovered above the ironmongery, you never knew what you might find that would be of use in the bakery or the shop. He bent over the low tables picking at this and that, then conscious that he might seem idle, he frowned as to suggest serious consideration was being given to important purchases.

But really, he did not have the energy he used to, he had just recently stopped waxing the tightly twirled ends of his moustache into fine points which he used to enjoy placing at a right angle to his nose.

He went off walking carefully on the cobble stones watching the lads load up the van outside the bakery. He still delighted in the smell of yeast and the proving loaves. He supposed it was one of his earliest memories for it reminded him of his father Robert, the first in a line of Loftus bakers which he hoped Max would carry on. But, worryingly, as yet there were no children to carry on the Race baking tradition.

And of course his second boy, Ernest, was off to chase his fortune in the colonies. Well he was a man now, served country and king in the Great War and came home. Which is all his mother wanted, his sisters too, what we all wanted.

There! He'd gone and forgotten his errand. Without a word he went back down dead-end road out into High St where all the shops either side had been set back time immemorial to make a market place. He paused, wondering what bit of lace or other frippery Sarah had asked him to get from Cammells. For her hat? Something for one of the girls? He looked again down North Rd on the corner at the familiar bay windows. Tudor style, he would have thought. But old CJ Dodds the draper was long gone. It was now the Loftus Working Men's Club and Institute.

W Maxwell remembered vividly the crowds outside Dodds low awning, pressing close to the windows at the Coronation. Before the War, the flags, bunting, the cries of 'long live the king!', and Britannia on a cart, long tresses and holding a sceptre. Food out on trestle tables, a bonfire which all the children came to see.

Now, of course, Dodds has his old ornate iron name above his new shop in Smithfield House. But the man had taken to using his, W Maxwell's, sign writer and even used the same font to add his name to the hoarding above the doorway. Still CJ Dodds is on a corner again. Better business that way. But he wasn't forgiving old CJ for copying his way of painting his name.

But when up that end of town visiting the other premises, he would always pop in for a chat, remember a few of the old times, before he went next door to Leng's for a trim and a wax.

But today it would be Cammells, just a few doors up, for some women's finery. The man sold undergarments. Cammells had, like the Races, been in Market Place forever. His father, Robert, set up shop a decade or so before old CT Cammell came along. Front St it was called in those days.

W Maxwell sighed. He was fated to have his name always linked to the proprietor of this enterprise. His, W Maxwell's enterprise, was the staff of life and Cammell's business was vanity, all vanity. The joke famous all about was that it was only here in Loftus that one could see a Race between a Cammell and Lion looked over by an Angel.

It was time to get back, he had been away ages. No idea what it was that Sarah had wanted. No matter, it had been a long morning. He put his hands on his hips and straightened his back and turned back homewards.

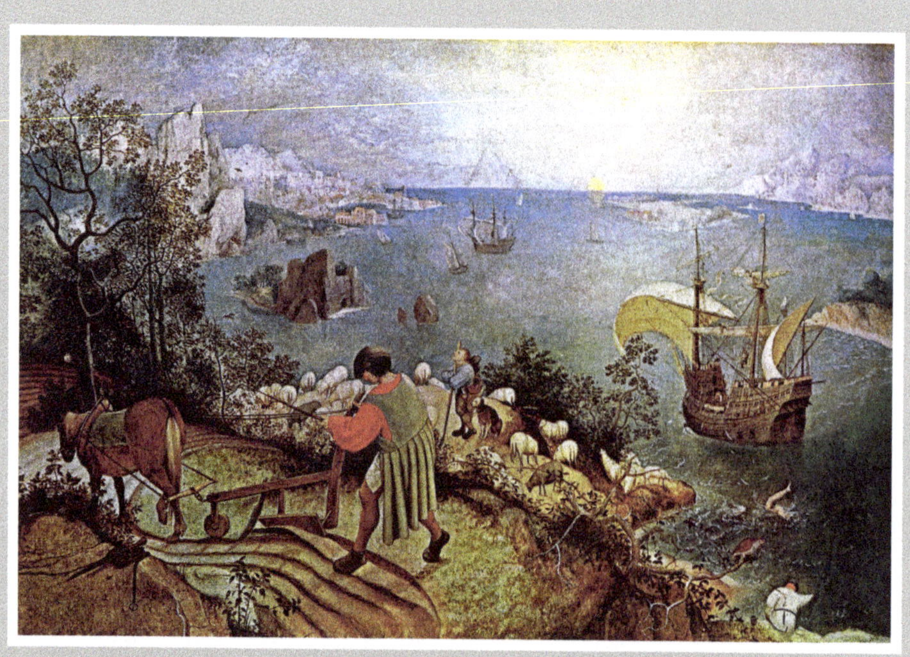

8

Landscape with the Fall of Icarus – Bruegel

There was a fashion in the late 1970s whereby a print was pasted directly onto a solid but light piece of wood. It was then sealed with a clear varnish. The image could be fastened to a wall without the need for a frame or glass.

This is how I mounted and displayed the photographic print of Bruegel's *Landscape with the Fall of Icarus*. With each new room in a new house I would carefully hang this picture where I could always catch sight of it.

I immediately liked the picture of Daedalus' son fallen from the sky. He had flown too close to the sun which melted the wax that held the feathers of his wings together. Bruegel fills his image with scenes of the rural life of his time. He depicts various farming activities and ships sailing out on the waters into which Icarus disappears.

In this illustration of Ovid's story he was applying his art to an ancient story. He sets this Greek myth in amongst the tiller, herdsman, and fisherman of his own 16th century Netherlands. I think it is the specificity of Bruegel's depiction of time and place that drew me first to his work. I was entranced by the peculiar feel of his landscapes, the perspective that could draw me shivering into a winter scene, or wanting to take off my coat and join his hay cutters on a summer's day.

It is something about Bruegel's manner that suggested immediately a truthfulness about the scenes he was depicting, the time and place of the Low Countries in the 1560s. It is not just the detail, the wooden wheel freeing the passage of the single wooden blade of the plough, or the patient pose of the shepherd's dog, but something in Bruegel's gaze that allowed me to enjoy a view of a time past in an almost photographic way.

It was much later that I learn that Bruegel's paintings were not only, or even, what the eye could see. The individually drawn leaves of the copse on the left may suggest the impersonal camera shutter but are carefully intended by an accomplished hand, and are a very personal part of the unfolding scene.

The particular attraction of this image was that the declared subject was not the ploughing of the field or the movement of a flock of sheep to greener pasture, let alone the fully rigged three-masted carrick heading out to open waters, but Icarus, only son of Daedalus, drowning after falling out of the sky. Without Bruegel's title most would struggle to make sense of the two legs, one silhouetted against the green water, the other foreshortened, pointing in our direction. No Daedalus, no feathered wings, no Crete.

No-one in the picture is paying any attention to what has happened, to the helpless figure disappearing beneath in the white-waved green water. It is just us, the viewer, who can take it all in, the sun-filled sky, the vast ocean ringed in pale peaked mountains, the ships growing smaller as they head out towards the horizon, the domesticated animals and their human handlers, a bird on a low branched shrub. It seems it is just us who realise that no help can be had for the young man drowning so far below us; that the time for a shout has passed, that we are caught in this moment. The tragedy of Daedalus and Icarus.

For, as hard as I try, I can't see this story of Daedalus and his son as an allegorical story of the dangers of pride. Pride before a fall: the Greek myth has been Christianised, made allegory for the sin of pleasure in success.

In Greek mythology hubris, a presumption, a pridefulness in the face of the gods, would bring Nemesis, a goddess, the agent of punishment. But there is no suggestion of this in the Roman Ovid. He has rustic bystanders catching sight of the flying figures, 'in astonishment, believing these creatures who could fly through the air must be gods'. A fair enough supposition but this is never what Daedalus intends or wishes.

In the centuries following the fall of Rome and the rise of Christianity, creation was considered the realm of the Christian God; only he could create. Man could but imitate, but the bringing forth, *ex nihilo*, belongs only to God. Man and his invention was suspect and brought the suspicion of pride which was always a sin against God.

I see Daedalus' story as a caution against invention; less for the act than unintended consequences. The story begins in King Minos' Crete and has several parts where Daedalus' power of invention is called upon. Firstly with Minos' queen Pasiphae bidding Daedalus to build a wooden cow so that she can mate with the bull that Poseidon had given the king as a sacrificial animal. The progeny of the coupling was the Minotaur, half-man half-bull, whose only form of sustenance was human flesh. Daedalus built the labyrinth to house and contain the beast.

Minos then imprisoned Daedalus and his son Icarus on Crete, it is not clear why; to protect the secret of the labyrinth perhaps and it is to escape this captivity that Daedalus settles on wings to bear both he and his son away for, as Ovid has Daedalus say: 'The king may block my way by land or across the ocean . . . but he does not possess the air.' It is this tragedy of escape that Bruegel re-tells within his picture of Brabant life.

Is it because I've known this picture most of my life that it presents such an intimate scene? The picture sweeps right to left, following behind the slightly hunched tiller as he guides his horse-drawn blade through the soft ground, the wavy grooves opening the red earth beneath the grass. His right foot is raised as if trying not to tread too hard on the furrows. His red sleeves draw us to the red blanket over the haunches of the patient horse going down the hill towards the copse of trees which lifts our gaze to rocky headlands that, pale and pink, lose their detail in the vast distance.

Land and sea are linked by the curve of the peasant's back echoed in the billowing spinnaker of the carrick sailing out between land into the open sea. Crowded between the ploughman and the ship is a fisherman throwing a line from the shore, a bird on a branch (looking like a turtle), and sheep graze while the herdsman, arms crossed, gazes upwards and, as a detail, Icarus disappears beneath the waves.

Bruegel draws all the elements of the scene into one coherent landscape suggesting a transient moment caught for all time in all its detailed uniqueness. The eternal but never to come again: it's the intimacy that Bruegel creates, the knowing of something we have never seen except through Bruegel's eyes.

But the paradox can be deepened: Bruegel, our trusted chronicler and imager has never seen just this scene himself. He has used fragments, part-scenes real and imagined to put together his landscape. His art more the novelist than the documentary maker. Brabantine perhaps, but the cliffs and precipices are not of his native Low Countries, the sunshine is Mediterranean and even the cast of characters performing the labour of Bruegel's time are taken from Ovid: 'Some fisher perhaps, plying his quivering rod, some shepherd leaning on his staff, or a peasant bent over his plough caught sight of them as they flew past.'

Only one of Bruegel's paintings depicts an actual locality. On his Italian journey he visited Naples and made sketches of the low hills and curving arms of the great harbour of Naples which he later did in oils. But in all the other paintings the towns, landscapes, and people, none are of a particular place or person. He never did a portrait (or a nude) and only once fulfilled a commission, and that was for a series of works showing the countryside in the different seasons of the year.

What I see and believe is a fiction of sorts: such as Anna Karenina, Raskolnikov, or the town of Middlemarch or Combray.

The Vasari of the north, Carel van Mander, relates in his lives of the artists, that Bruegel and his friend joined in the peasant life disguised as rustics. At weddings, 'they bought gifts like the other guests ... Bruegel delighted in observing ... the peasants, how they ate, danced, drank, capered or made love.'

So this man we trust comes to us in disguise, he is as pretend, perhaps, as his pictures. As someone once said of Vivaldi's *Four Seasons*, it was 'a townies take' on the countryside.

Still, there is no question that the world depicted in Bruegel's pictures is the world he lived in. It is his vision that envelopes us, the impossible vistas created out of imagination, perhaps distant memories of his Alpine crossing. He invokes a flexible perspective that brings objects, people, scenes, closer or further from one another as his wish dictates. And for us, his wish is that we really see, and believe in his world.

While Bruegel did only one painting from myth he painted many scenes from the Bible and I think there is a clue in some of these works as to why he depicted the fall of Icarus in the way that he did.

In *Christ Carrying the Cross* we see a great sweep of Bruegel's people, the local militia out on horseback, helmeted and carrying pikes, villagers on foot and horseback, children on their parents' shoulders, all winding their way up to the local commons where a crowd already encircles Golgotha.

The whole town has turned out for the spectacle. The picture frames them with gibbets and torture wheels on either side; the ground is churned up, horses feet stick in the mud, rugged up against the cold, but none will be deterred, the crucifixion awaits them on the hill.

Again it takes us some time to find the ostensible subject of this scene, the reason for this picnic on the village commons. But Christ is here. He has stumbled under the heavy cross while his co-condemned ride in a horse drawn cart ahead of him. Trees are in leaf, crows are carried on the cold air as clouds come up from the horizon. Late spring perhaps?

As everyone performs their role here on a chilly Brabant afternoon, so does our Christ, set about by his tormentors who, even now, not wishing to delay the show, attempt to lift the cross so to facilitate Christ's continued progression up the hill to the waiting villagers.

Auden in his poem 'Musée des Beaux Arts' talks about 'the old masters' being never wrong about suffering. That they knew its human position. He instances Bruegel's *Landscape with the Fall of Icarus* suggesting the old master's depiction was a scene of suffering to which all observers could not but be indifferent: 'how everything turns away/ Quite leisurely from the disaster'.

But I'm not sure this is Bruegel's intent at all. I think his concern was to suggest the eternal verity of the scene: his observers are not indifferent but accepting. If they notice, it is silently, disinterestedly, with a keen appreciation of the necessity of all acts at all times.

Indeed, as they fish, plough, or lean on a staff, so does Christ fall beneath his cross, and Icarus disappear into the cold green seawater.

Icarus' fall is not something existing outside time and place but forever embedded in whatever time and place a painter is given to depict, wants to place us. It is Bruegel's mastery at providing us with a particular time and place, something specific, a locality; it is Bruegel's detail in his lifelikeness which confirms Icarus' place and moment – defining the moment as now, but the act as eternal.

Bruegel's Icarus is an event, a story, that is always happening, like the suffering of Christ and, like the bread and wine of the Mass, not a metaphor but truly a transubstantiation; that Icarus, once fallen, is always, in all places, at all times, falling. We hear the splash and, knowing all this, plough on, set our sails, and muse while the flock grazes.

9

What is a Photograph?

I often find myself asking: what is photograph? But I do not ask what is a water colour or a pen and ink sketch or even a print from an etched plate or woodblock. What is it that I understand about these latter images that I do not understand about a photograph?

Is it to do with a perceived difference in manufacture? Or perhaps with the quality of the resulting image or perhaps its reproducibility.

Or someone might say looking at a photo of a room in a house: that is how it looks, meaning that's what this room really looks like. But of course the same could be said of a painted picture of a room. By the same token we could say of both representations that neither look like the room; that we know the room, and it does not look like how it is depicted in both the painting and photograph.

For both the painted picture and photograph, the image is something selected. The image is a manufacture. Perhaps the photograph hides the marks of its creation in a way a painting, or sketch, or print from an engraved plate doesn't? But of course it may still be possible to say of a photograph: that is by Nadar or Sandor or Cartier-Bresson; or like a pencil sketch: I remember the artist drawing that.

Consider the process of manufacture of an etching. The plate is covered in wax then the engraver uses a needle to draw the lines of the image in the wax, scraping the wax away to expose the metal plate below. Then the plate is dipped in the *mordant*, the acid which bites into the exposed plate creating the lines which will comprise the image when printed.

The plate is covered in ink some of which fills the multiple incised lines, thin and thick, tapered and blunt, single, or cross hatched in the metal plate. This etched plate is akin to the photograph negative. And the surface is then wiped clean so that the paper pressed against it just picks up the ink left in the incisions.

I compare this to the photographic process and attempt to align both images' manufacture. The camera film is coated by light sensitive silver halide crystals in a gelatine emulsion. The camera's lens controls the exposure of the film to light reflected off objects in front of the lens. However, there are many settings that can be altered both at the level of the film itself (light sensitivity) and at the time of exposure in the camera: shutter aperture, speed, ISO setting. Then (I am talking here of black and white photography) at the time of processing the negative, the time of immersion in the developer, the temperature of the solution, then the fixing and drying of the negatives. All these parts of the process can be subject to variation as dictated by the photographer.

If I look at an etching by Rembrandt, it is clear that he has decided on where the shadows fall, which ones are darker than others, what details are to be picked out, what will be illuminated by the strong light, etc.

It might be objected that the photographer is passive in the face of what the day has chosen to illuminate in the landscape the photographer wishes to capture on film. Well, so too, Rembrandt. But both are faced with a similar scene and lighting, and both are able to select, emphasise, overlook, adjust and compose the scene in front of them to create an effect that is marked by their intentions or vision if you prefer.

So, the room I do not quite recognise in the photograph is still that room but created anew by the photographer's craft and intentions.

* * *

The photograph of my grandmother – I look at it and say that is my grandmother. A small painted portrait of someone is described as 'a likeness of Mrs –'.

A photograph of a landscape – it is as if it has question marks about it. A Constable is, but a photograph of the landscape is, 'as it were'.

The issue is not just one of manufacture but of manipulation – the creator's intention, the purpose.

Holiday snaps to remember the moment – but who is remembering – me, or the photograph?

What do I want to recall? What is it I want access to? What is it I can't let go?

There is something to be remembered but, really, it is unreachable.

* * *

Perhaps in looking at a photograph there is a misapprehension. Some slippage that puts both the viewer and the viewed on a false footing, and from which follows a cascade of misunderstanding, a falling into bad faith. Something invisible yet inevitable.

And, at the end, none is any the wiser, on the contrary something that might have been known is lost. That vast well of ignorance has been added to – a few more drops of willed and innocent unknowing.

Perhaps the painting, the sketch, is so foreign, so seemingly in need of translation, of explanation, of elucidation that, not for a moment, do I believe in it – not for an instant am I fooled into forgetting what it is I know about this place.

There is an instant falsity in my reading of a photograph that is impossible with other forms of manufactured image. And perhaps this is why the photograph will always be seen as inferior, as an impersonation, while what I have to work at so hard to make sensible, visible, and comprehendible will always be regarded as the 'true likeness', the real portrait, the true-to-life landscape.

I am ashamed before a photograph in a way I never am before a painting, something so obviously handmade.

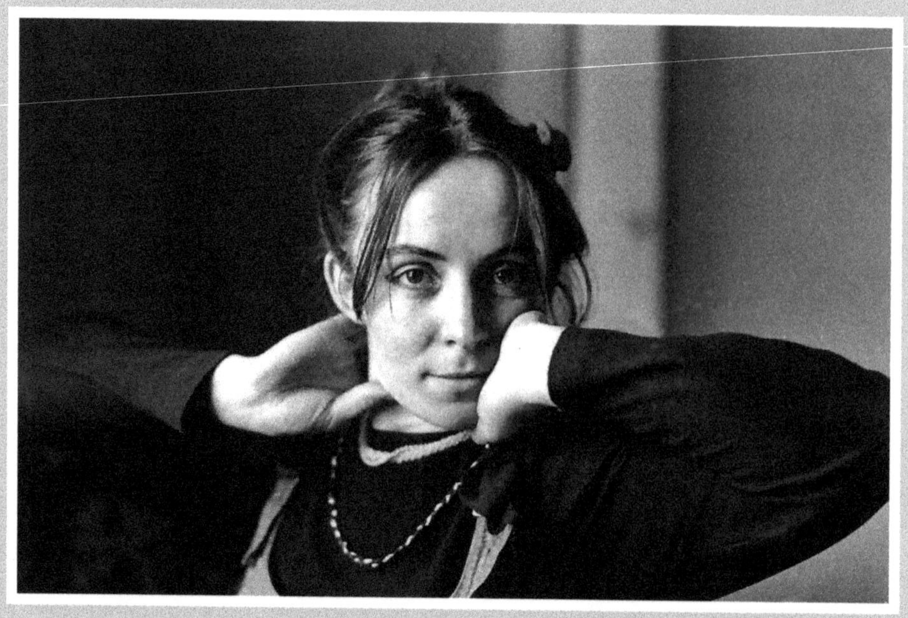

10

Young Woman

This is a picture of my neighbour. It was taken some 37 years ago in the winter of 1982. A bad winter, I remember we had a power blackout one day, the first I ever experienced in the suburb of the big city where I lived at the time.

I was a student and had little furniture. My bed was on a futon base close to the floor. One morning in this bad winter I awoke. I could hear a scratching, I thought it might be a bare branch against the window pane. But then I opened my eyes on the pillow and looked across the room. A large rat was scratching his pale nails at the skirting board. It looked briefly over its shoulder at me before shaking its whiskers and returning all its attention to the board.

A cold winter and, in all this, Brezhnev died. An event. He had been the President of the USSR for most of my life, his was the face of the Cold War, dark eyebrows, a set jaw, his finger was on the nuclear button: nothing happened under his rule, the USSR and its satellite countries behind the Iron Curtain all stagnated.

I shared the half-house with a red-haired writer. I had known him for a few years. We played cards together in a group of writers, and one day he suggested we share a place. It was an old house, but solid brick in the style of the southern suburbs. There was a tram stop just down the road which would be useful, as I was dependent on public transport to get to the university and to work.

I can't remember because it was so long ago, but did I lay rat poison? *Ratsack* was it called? But anyway, some days after I saw the rat in my bedroom, I discovered a dead rat in the toilet bowl. Had it drowned? Had the poison done its work?

I was doing a degree at the university on the other side of the city. I was in my third year of a three-year arts degree but I wasn't doing well.

And I had misunderstood the arrangement I had with H about the house. Or he didn't explain it at all but, when he moved in, there was no bed, no clothing: just a table, books, bookcases and a chair. He never spent a night in his room, nor ate a meal in the kitchen.

I don't remember being very surprised; we all spent a lot of our lives in counterfactual worlds in those days. I was just disappointed that I would be, in the end, sharing so little with my housemate.

I had a little electric bar radiator, whose curved reflecting surface was spotted with rust. I put it under the big table where I studied. The table and a small bookcase was all that was in the large room on the inside of the front door. H's room was on one side of this big room and, opposite, a hallway ran to my bedroom then opened onto a wall-papered kitchen. There was a back door and short flight of rickety wooden steps that descended to a back yard.

The evenings were quiet – just me and Bruce Springsteen's *The River*, and then later when I went to bed it was quieter still.

So it was easy for me to hear the dog in the night. I was used to the sound of the late trams hurtling down the wide main road. But the dog did not fade away, did not slip silent on sand and come to a halt. I had a black planet lamp on the floor by the bed, I could swivel it and throw strange shadows on the high walls when I awoke to the cold, or the sound of that dog. Barking then howling: barking and barking at something.

I knew a bit about dogs, my previous girlfriend had one. Dogs bark because of something specific, it is not done for its own sake. And I could hear, hear the intent in the voice of this dog, somewhere close, barking intently at all hours of the black night.

It worried me that I was getting behind in my work. Each year of my course, it seemed, I lost my way a little more. I was studying the history and philosophy of science: I had learnt a lot about Darwin and evolutionary science, some quantum mechanics, and had philosophised about 'paradigm shifts': plate tectonics, chaos theory. But, this year, I missed out on a unit I had wanted to study and now was doing a unit in another faculty, Middle Eastern Studies.

I had been reading a scholar whose life-long study had been Renaissance magic: I was deep into Hermeticism, and understood Giordano Bruno was an out-and-out sorcerer. I was following the arcane methods of medieval alchemy and the kabala with books I bought from the Theosophical Society bookshop.

I had to find out where the dog was and why it barked so intently, so despairingly. One night I went down the rickety wooden back steps following the barking. The dog was next door over a wooden paling fence. A big black dog, some sort of cross with hairy pointed ears. I could see him from the height of the back steps; in next door's backyard, barking at the house, where there were lights showing.

✱ ✱ ✱

As it turned out, I only saw H, the writer, for a half-hour or so between when he knocked off from wiring up industrial air-conditioners in a factory and when he went to write on the big desk in his room. We would share a few beers, a few cigarettes, a story or two. He worked at the house for a few hours then left punctually at 6.30 to go home and have dinner with his mother with whom he lived.

One bright and sunny day I went into the street where the trams sung along the wires and cars skidded across the shiny embedded steel tracks. I went down the driveway of the house next door. I understood that the dog barked when the occupants were at home. But who these people were I had no idea. Nor did I really want to find out.

I knocked on the wire door and stepped down and back as I heard the front door open. A woman's voice demanded to know what I wanted, what I was doing there. She spoke through the wire door. I tried to explain about the dog and my disturbed sleep. She paused, and opened the wire door a little, looked at me and then glanced up the driveway to the road.

'You come in', she ordered, stepping back. 'You talking about my Willy? He is good dog. I am on my own. I need it dog.'

I stood in the hallway and looked around. 'What are you looking at?' she asked angrily. 'What you doing here?' I spoke again about the dog; said I was a student, that perhaps she could let the dog in and it wouldn't bark so much. 'How you know about me? You go now. I not know what you want', and she pushed open the wire door. But her tone of voice had changed and, as I ducked past her, she shook her head very slightly.

By day I studied the 'double-slit experiment' whereby light was shown to be both a particle and a wave at the same time; it was a question of observation. Then in the evening I wondered at the movement of crows in the bare branches, divination is possible, but do I dare? Bruno thought Copernicus had missed the point with his mathematics, did not understand the true power of astral magic of the microcosm and the macrocosm; the inquisition knew what they were about burning Bruno: all magic was diabolical.

I went back of course. The dog still barked but M gave me a cup of tea. She was Polish and her English was very patchy. We worked out a possible solution: when she was home and she didn't want Willy inside, she could let him into a small back porch: at once inside and outside.

Through our conversations, which took a long time because of translation problems, I learnt she worked by day at a geriatric hospital on the other side of the city. On her lunch break she watched 'my serials' on TV. *The Bold and The Beautiful, Days of Our Lives*, or napped. I met the dog, a big German Shepherd, crossed with something else: I was relieved to get my rest at night.

The pipes froze that winter. I fished the rat out of the toilet and wrapped it in newspaper. Its protruding upper front teeth made it look comical bound up in news of road fatalities, public transport fare hikes, and flash floods.

Then one morning I woke late and knew I would miss my exam on Babylonian king lists, in Middle Eastern Studies. I wouldn't complete my degree this year.

M took me to Polish House where I had piroshky and saw how at home she was speaking Polish with the other diners. Occasionally she came by and I would cook her a meal.

One day H came in around 4.30 pm as he usually did, and complained that he had been here that morning and found all the dishes and glasses undone, dirty on the table and sink. He was angry, saying that it was his house and who was living here anyway?

Sometimes I would hear Willy bark at night and I could hear M's voice coming from the driveway near her front door. She was shouting at someone. But Willy stopped barking, so she must have let him into the back porch once she went inside.

We both lived in half-houses, both in halfway houses to someplace else. We both worked as cleaners in hospitals to pay our way.

After a while H didn't want to pay his half of the rent anymore. The weather warmed up and we did not renew the lease. I managed to finish my degree the following year. The photograph was taken on a day when M came to visit me.

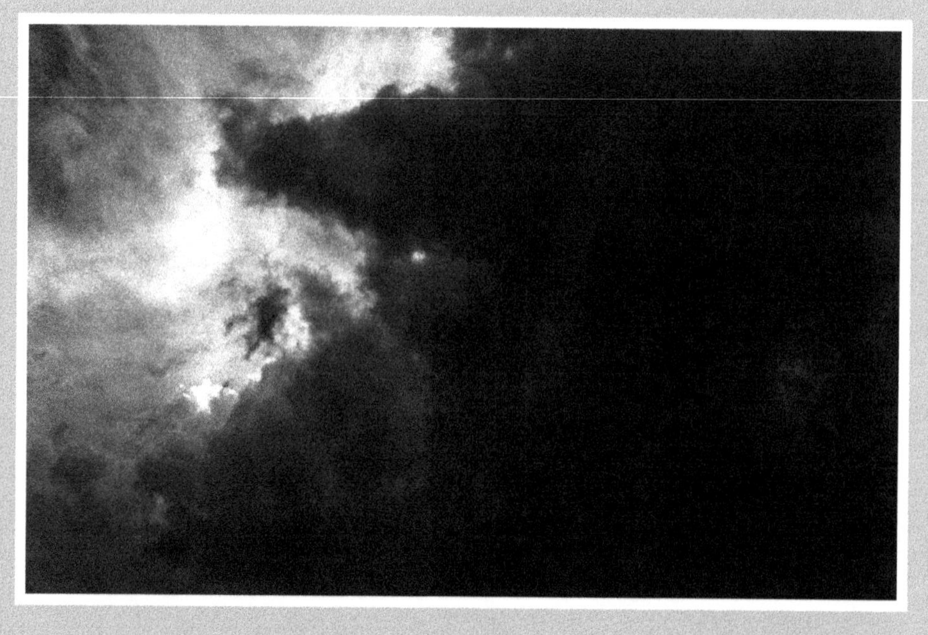

11

Storm Cloud

This is a picture of a storm blowing in from the north west, one early afternoon. The sky was blue, glazed with washes of wispy curling thin white cloud. High up, everything was high up, the dome of sky, a thin eggshell at the edge of space.

Then this low cloud, dark and heavy appeared moving slowly, the anvil of Thor protruding from its side. Thick, absorbing, blocking out the light of the invisible sun, heavy dark grey, thickening to a soupy purple, suddenly lumbering up from the flat horizon, a voluminous sheet sliding slowly, inexorably into position between the land and sky. Unhurried, it kept its strange shape as it shrank the people, houses and animals beneath, while making the sky even more unreachable, unattainable. Bright, streaked, blue and white, the edge of everything became eclipsed. An eye, full of light, once seeing across land, mountains and seas, was being occluded.

This dark cloud with its blunt wedge pressing ahead seemed unlike the clouds whose shape was always changing, roiling and disintegrating only to reform as something else.

Turbulence, the mathematics of which no eye can contemplate for long, wishing instead for a geometry of mountain slopes, dotted bitumen dwindling to a point out at the horizon. Turbulence, which tells us of molecules madly swirling, energetic, entropic, effervescent.

So this cloud marches in, all polished leather and hard edged, an army whose formation is directed from above, from unseen forces it wishes would rule for all its unruly life.

It is a winter storm come to lash the tops of tall gums, laminate the smooth roads and paths with a continuously replenished sheen of water. It marches overhead and I am standing beneath it looking up with my camera. I wonder what it is I should photograph, wonder, as I always do, what it is I am looking at, wonder at what composition, what framing will release me from my anxiety. But really we are hapless, my camera and I, both looking one to the other to call the shots.

There is nothing to be found in all these clouds, this water vapour, ice crystals, nothing to be seen except what an eye can imagine.

High in the troposphere the cirrus forms a blank canvas onto which the low cumulus force themselves, a sharp cut-out shadow play; creating a shape to cover over the solid things of the earth. I stand down here not knowing how to look at what I am seeing; waiting for the camera to raise my forearm, move my left hand in front of my face, cover my eye, my cheek, shadow me under its solid weight, and I look through a glass eye, all refraction, mirrors and moving ground glass. Take me, take me.

Sunlight above forces its way down into the dark cloud, the enveloping mass has thin spots where the sun penetrates tuning the darkness with softer edges, adding blue to the mix. A patch lower right, some shape to discern in the shapeless mass of the underside of this rain-laden cloud.

A pulse of bluish-red, like an unborn imaged by ultrasound, a pulse of a heart; perhaps not creaturely at all, the aegis of a god, at once alive and utterly indifferent.

It doesn't matter. The confection of water molecules and heat has nearly covered the whole sky. The bright day shedding shadows beneath trees and telephone poles, follows me as I lengthen with the passing hours – all this has gone. A winter storm – an army implacable with a single heart; a smudge that just plays at rhythm, fools my eye, the lens opening and closing as I move the camera here and there, trying to find what it is I am to photograph.

* * *

Clouds are not really a very easy subject to photograph. Massed, they can lack shape and definition. A cloud needs to be isolated, separated out with light and dark from the skyscape surrounding it.

A band of cloud on the horizon can look just like a band of cloud on the horizon. But, closer, it can be composed, framed and given presence. When the sun is bright, sharp shadows carve its features into a subject.

Many photographed clouds are not as striking as the one here. There is drama in terms of the light and dark and also in the intimation of a violent change.

Sky and cloud, a layering of shapes and a little colour, the photo creates a subject discrete and apart out of the ubiquitous and impermanent.

I read a book on clouds once. A taxonomy of clouds, sensible, logical, based on altitude, wind and moisture. Cumulonimbus, cirrostratus, nimbostratus.

There was something else that could be said about clouds but this book seemed unaware of this, a sort of wilful ignorance that shocked me. I soon gave the book away.

Some of my pictures of clouds were put in an exhibition. People who came to look at them walked up and down in front of the big prints, turning their heads this way and that. Some, after doing this for awhile, would remark with some satisfaction that 'this cloud was like a big dog', or 'that was just like a ferris wheel', or 'I see waves on a rocky shore'. Sometimes a viewer would suggest what the cloud looked like to them, then turn to me as if for some confirmation, or smile as if to say I had been found out, or indeed that they had winkled the truth from close and lengthy observation.

Of course I have done something like this in the earlier part of my description with my talk of gods and armies. Have I found myself out? Or is it that the compulsion to narrate overcomes a sense that all is mist and vapour? And that the meteorologists' taxonomy is a fair description after all? An attempt to describe without invention?

In truth, I like the sharply delineated shapes of the lower cloud and the space between it and the blue and white sky. I like the composition that suggests that soon, even the top left will be obscured by dense cloud, and that soon no light will be let in.

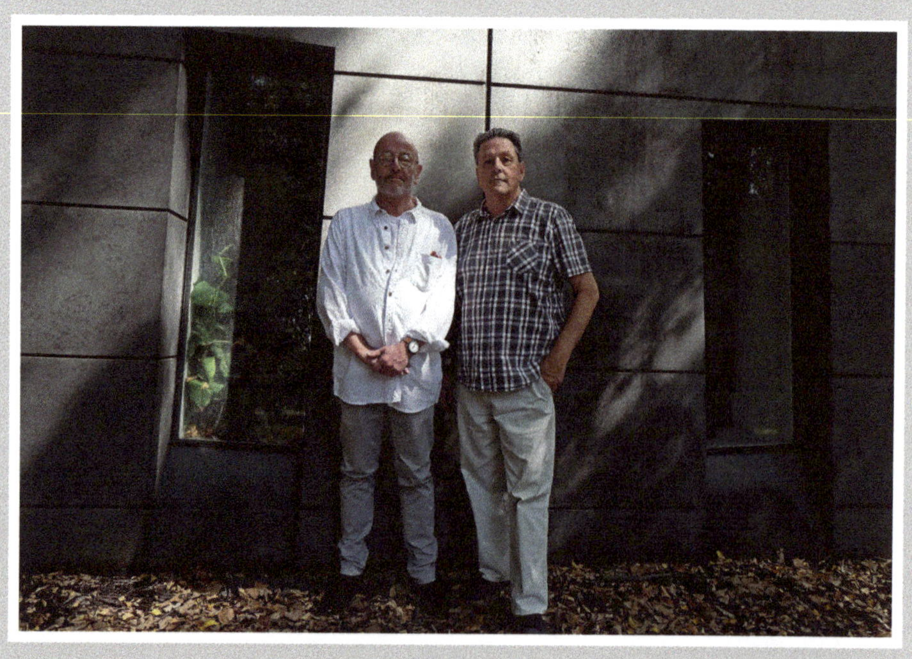

12

Two Old Friends

This is a beautifully hand coloured photograph taken some time ago now. The actual date is unknown, but on the back is stamped 'M & E – cover?'. It has been suggested that the picture was intended to be used on the cover of a joint memoir the two old hoofers were writing.

Those whose interest is in light entertainment and theatrics will perhaps recognise the once passably famous (their expression) Marcel and Ernesto. They are almost unrecognisable now out of costume, but the slight turn of lip and arched eyebrow, are enough to call up memories of these vaudevillians of long ago.

Marcel and Ernesto, both from Yorkshire, met on the boards as teenagers and by the time of this photo had known each other for almost fifty years. Most of those years they trod the boards of innumerable Tivolis throughout the country. There were few acts that they did not try in the music halls that thrived in those years when they entertained us: soft shoe, comedy, slapstick, juggling, and of course the act that made them famous for a few months, and which is still talked about: the ventriloquist act that made their fortune.

This short piece has been compiled from some old 78rpm shellac recordings, recently discovered at a country auction and several cassette tapes that seem to be a recording of a series of radio interviews. The memoir for which the photo was presumably taken has not surfaced and extensive research would suggest that it was never written.

This piece is far from comprehensive, as if such a thing could be, but if it adds even a few details to people's memories and recollections of M & E and the heady days of vaudeville, then the author's efforts will not be regarded as wasted.

Marcel, on the left in this picture, was a north country lad born just near Whitby on the coast. His father was a miner who reportedly had a fine baritone voice and was in great demand at weddings and other local festivities. It is said that his heart was broken when it became clear that Marcel was tone deaf and couldn't string a tune together. The final straw came when Marcel failed a yodelling course that his father, at some expense, had arranged. It is said the pair never spoke until Mark, his father, bequeathed Marcel his collection of piano rolls which he thought would provide his son with a nest egg to be called on when the boy discovered that he was indeed good for nothing.

One irony is that it is through one of these rolls that we can still hear Marcel's voice as he recorded some his comic routines for posterity.

Ernesto's father was a baker but, as soon as Ernesto was old enough, he ran away with the circus. It was a flea circus and, however much he tried, Ernesto said 'I could never get the arthropods to accept me as one of their own.'

So from the outset the boys struggled to find a life of their own; it was one of the things that brought them together: a desire to make everything up from scratch. Marcel is a stage name, and Ernesto is a nickname because, as Marcel quips on tape: 'He is hysterically sincere.'

They started their theatrical life together by teaching one another the soft shoe shuffle. They broke into the local Working Men's

Institute Hall with bags of sand gathered by the seashore to practice. It was suggested by appreciative reviews that this gave them the life-long ability to intuit where the other was at any given time on the stage, invaluable for juggling and song and dance routines.

While their fame was not universal, and then only for a few months, after which their careers looked all but over, they often regaled their fans with stories of the powerful and famous they had met in their years of touring: 'Buster Beckett, strong Irish accent, never heard in his silent work, trains, cars, marvellous stuff, timing was perfect. "Endgame", "Krapps Last Tape", very short routines, no sound at all. Timing perfect, "Mercier and Camier" could have been written about us, eh Ernie? But he got serious with a capital "S" (guffaws of laughter on tape) with the opera, "Waiting for God Knows Who"!' (tape ends with both laughing hysterically and breaking into a rendition of the popular song, *How can they tell I'm Irish?*).

Now we must turn to the vent act that no doubt many reading these pages will be familiar with. It is what put the hitherto small time artistes on the map.

Nothing in their previous work gave any inkling of the *tour de force* of the act that fused the two performers into one. The notices gave the act the title 'ME!' and the audience was left to separate out the two letters into Marcel and Ernesto if they could, or if they were able to.

Briefly, Marcel came out 'carrying' Ernesto, his dummy, before settling him on his knee, and then, threw his voice to create a dialogue ad libbed between two friends who had worked and lived the same world with all its vicissitudes for many years. The repartee was sparkling 'between' the ventriloquist and his emaciated, motionless dummy, whose facial movements were the only thing that animated the painted face.

It may have been the novelty of the act or perhaps something to do with the fact that, despite seeming wooden and motionless except for the actions of Marcel, it was in fact a human sitting bonily on Marcel's padded knees.

Whatever it was, the audiences took a few moments to see the great promise, the great humour and fun to be had as the two old hands put themselves through their paces on the sawdust covered floor.

But word of mouth soon had operators and impresarios knocking at management's door wanting the new sensation in their halls, taverns and theatres. Up and down the country Marcel and Ernesto went making money for everyone including, it is said, themselves. An unheard of deal *diablo* meant their cut was an astronomical amount for the time, and for a pair of hitherto jobbing specialist artistes.

It was only much later, after the furore over the sudden pulling of the act died down, that details began to emerge of the price paid by the now unemployable performers for their greatest success.

Marcel and Ernesto were both essentially comedians who became drawn to vaudeville because, as an art form, it was not interested in the psychology of the acts nor in 'improving' the public who came to pay and applaud them. This lack of insight and a complete absence of morality meant that, when the end came for M & E, it was not really thinkable, and words could not really be found for such a calamity. But after a lifetime of quick turnarounds, pratfalls and continuous rhythmical banter, silence was not an option.

If there was to be no song and dance there was to be nothing at all.

When seen together in later years they were doing a soft shoe shuffle or singing a ditty long out of fashion. The juggling of stacks of plates was long gone (an early attempt to do this with infants failed because, almost immediately, they began to throw up). As they grew older, they no longer had the breath for the kazoo, and an accident with a soup bowl had put Marcel's ukulele playing days behind him. But it was said that when they trod the boards under the lights they could still depend on that sixth sense that meant that together they could perform any chosen choreography perfectly.

It was only by reading between the lines and picking up information from doctors' charts and nurses well-meaning gossip that it is possible to have some detail of the unholy deal they made that ensured that fleeting country-wide fame.

Was it Bell's Palsy or a stroke? No matter, Ernesto became paralysed, one side of his face and body. For awhile he was able to hide it with one-arm antics and thick grease paint but soon the helplessness in Marcel's face convinced Ernesto that he had to exit left.

Needing to put food on the table, Marcel teamed up with others who needed a foil or a fool to complete their act. Ernesto found laudanum, it relieved the pain and even relaxed the rictus of his face. Was it opium that finally addicted him? He no longer went out and began wasting away: no medical man could induce him to eat, to feel life was worth continuing. Cachectic and almost speechless, Ernesto was wasting away in front of a despairing Marcel.

Who stumbled upon the idea for the vent act no-one now wants to know. But it was decided. No makeup was needed except to put tuberculotic roses on each of the skin-and-bone cheeks of the 'dummy'. Ernesto's emaciation meant that the lines running down either side of the mouth were already in place and his light weight meant that Marcel could comfortably manage him for long periods sitting on his carefully padded thighs.

The rest, as they say, is history. It is remarkable that they both survived, as the picture before us attests. Their later life bears only a few sentences. Marcel became a cook and Ernesto drove parcel vans. There was a wife or two and children denied. Later in life, as pensioners, they shared a flat in Elsternwick filled with the memorabilia of their life on the stage.

It is a picture of two survivors, and although the photo suffers from being heavily re-touched, some of their colourful past can still be glimpsed in the flaking paint.

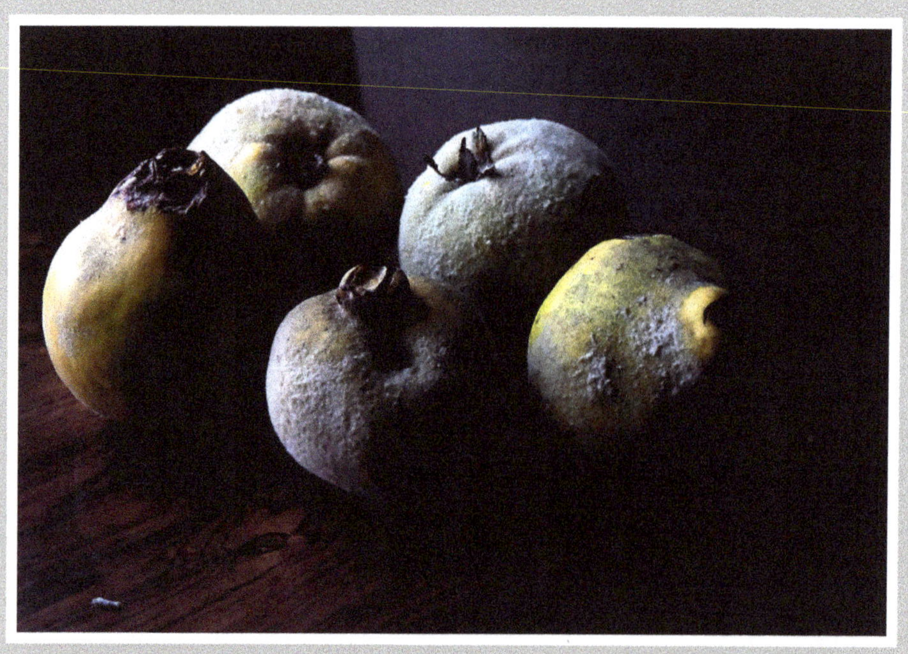

13

Five Pieces of Fruit

I found these five fruit in a bowl in the kitchen and took them into the workroom. I put them on the rosewood table near the window. I moved them about; no position made sense, there could be no rationale for any particular placement.

I was impatient, with little confidence that anything would work out. I moved things away with the back of my hand, elbowing everything aside. In the end I left the fruit just where they lay.

The fruit sat there as if growing out of the rosewood laminate; very soon I was helpless to even consider any other arrangement; I became the one who passed with the movement of the sun, coming and going at night and in the morning. The shadows around the fruit stayed close, and told no time but their own.

I made all my settings on the camera manual, hovered in some fractious orbit, navigated by eye and the twirling of knobs. It took me awhile to disappear from view.

* * *

Five shapes all complete and self-contained; joined, couched by the shadows that curve them, distinguished one from another. To me they all 'face' slightly different directions – they do not much include one another, but are not to be separated.

Their skins all differ; the light, variation in age, position on the tree, did they fall or were they picked from the tree? There is an intensity in the way they all appear, perhaps suddenly, perhaps one by one.

We look for clues. We always look for clues. Clues to what, we would be embarrassed to even speculate. Every mystery is an insult; each perceived clue is an admission. There is a little blue object in the foreground. The quince on the left is black with decay at its tapered end. The fur is grainy and a bluish colour. How big are these pieces of fruit? There is nothing else here except the quince.

I come into the workroom and see the fruit on the edge of the rosewood table which is held up by four lions' paws, resting surely on the carpet. I can see the fruit and the light, coming through the transparent white curtains, from the low sun in the north. I become invisible to myself, sitting close to this still life.

Taking pictures, considering the dark out of which, one by one, they come to be seen. It is their job to ensure my presence, the pictures are just for me – they require nothing: do their shadows cast my shape too?

I take my pictures, most of them are the same, I can see nothing different about them at all. One after the other, twisting, twirling, blinking, squinting; I enjoy the brief moments when the five fruit supplant me, become the only shadowed flesh in this room lit just with the low winter sun.

Some of the things on the table that once I pushed away I now bring back. I take pictures of the quinces with a blue bottle, with a jigsaw, with old rose petals. I admit my foolishness in the titles I give them: 'Quinces with blue bottle', 'Quinces with jigsaw and blue bottle', 'Quinces blue bottle rose petals'.

It makes no difference to the fruit, it brings nothing else out, there is nothing to be elicited by putting these things near the quince. After awhile I took all these things away again.

* * *

What makes things what they are? We search for clues in where they come from and how they are known to us. The Akkadians cultivated the quince throughout the empire on the fertile plains lying between the great rivers of Mesopotamia. This fruit grew much better than the apple in the dry air. The quince was known by them as 'supurgilla' over four thousand years ago.

The quince survived the collapse of the kingdoms of Akkad, of Babylonia and Sumer. The Arabs knew this fruit as 'safarjal' and in Hebrew it was known as 'perishin'. The difficulties of translation and transcription mean that, in ancient writings, the names given the hardy quince may have designated the apple as well. Though the suggestion that the quince was the fruit of the tree of knowledge of good and evil is, I think, fanciful. Eve would have spat out the astringent tough flesh before even tasting the mystical properties of this fruit.

The name given to it by modern science, the Linnaean classification, is *Cydonia oblonga*. The second word suggests a description of what we can sometimes see, the fruit is not round but distended, and oblong is a good word to describe this deviation from the sphere. *Cydonia* is more historical: it was a city in ancient Crete which grew a superior variety of quince tree according to the Greeks. They grafted the Cydonian wood to their rootstock. Thus the Greek name for this was the Cydonian melon (a word also connoting apple) or the melimelon (honey apple).

Years later Pliny the Elder, a Roman, in his Natural History says of the quince, 'the fruit is called by us "contonea", by the Greeks "Cydonia" and first introduced from the island of Crete.' The Latin name is apparently just a corruption of the Greek name 'Cydonia'. So the quince leaves its origins in central Asia and Mesopotamia and moves via Crete to Greece and Rome.

Do I begin to see a glimmer of the image that is before me now? Do I begin to know the quince? Perhaps the scent now begins to waft up from the shiny skin or tufts of curled 'hair'.

We are very close: the Old French plural of *quoyn* is a few steps away from the bowed tree laden with ripe fruit for the harvesting. There: the five pieces lie on the rosewood table. Do I know them now? Know them for what they are?

Of what then are they composed? Of the lists I consult, I learn that a quince is ninety-five percent water, with a little carbohydrate, even less Vitamin C (not enough to ward off scurvy), and has traces of magnesium, phosphorous, and potassium. No mention of what gives its colour, no mention of the nature of the curly fuzz that appears when maturing.

I who eat the quince know the granular, dry flesh; when cut, no juice pours out or even wets my knife. This is nothing like a pear or an apple. The quince has a fleeting scent, not pungent like an apple nor silky sweet as the pear.

The quince is tough to cut, to pare away the seeds and white surrounds. It is often cooked with a great amount of sugar to mitigate its 'sourness'. It is sometimes doused in lemon juice to stop it oxidising and turning brown.

Do I now at last know what it is, this quince of mine? The single member of the genus, *Cydonia oblonga*, this graft from a Cretan city, this misshapen globe?

I know its names, its history, the ingredients, the places where it is grown and by whom. But is that what is on the table, and now in this photograph? No, none of it.

If you like, the unknown remains. It is just the specifics of these particular pieces of fruit that I am left with, and not even that – just a photo of the fruit, all past their prime, to be sure, but still absolutely what they are.

The weighty, furry and shiny smooth fruit, enveloped by a thick and sinking scent, are all gone. As they sat in the cool workroom these quinces were slowly being consumed by bacteria and fungi. These bodies all the time decomposing as I hovered above them, wishing for a little more light and dark so that they might give up what I was wanting to know from them.

The single tree growing in the back yard is four years old. We built a frame of wooden poles and curved conduit over the top. It reached up some fifteen feet. The frame we draped with white netting, staked tight into the ground.

The tree blossomed in October. Hundreds of frail white petals formed at the ends of the twigs and branches. Hundreds of little fruit grew and over the weeks this green fruit, the size of a thumb, fell onto the uncut lawn beneath the tree. I counted each one as I collected them up.

In the end there were left 35 fruit that continued to grow and mature. In late May they ripened; I picked them from the branches or from the ground where they fell. This fruit was just the size of my fist, the skin was smooth under the grey-blue fuzz. These quince were not gnarled or deeply furrowed like some fruit in the shop. I don't know the name of the variety I grew.

I used the cored, peeled and sliced quince in tarts, in addition to, or as a replacement for apples. I made apple and quince crumble, quince crumble cake, and a quince and almond cream tart. Often I just stewed them lightly with a little water and sugar. The colour of the cooked flesh was a little pink, but not a bright colour nor ruby red. I ate the stewed quince with yoghurt. I put them in pies and made jam. The thirty-five fruit were more than enough. I did not make quince paste, nor did I bake them.

These five were left when all the others had been eaten. They went into the compost barrels when it was clear that taking another photograph would be of no help to me.

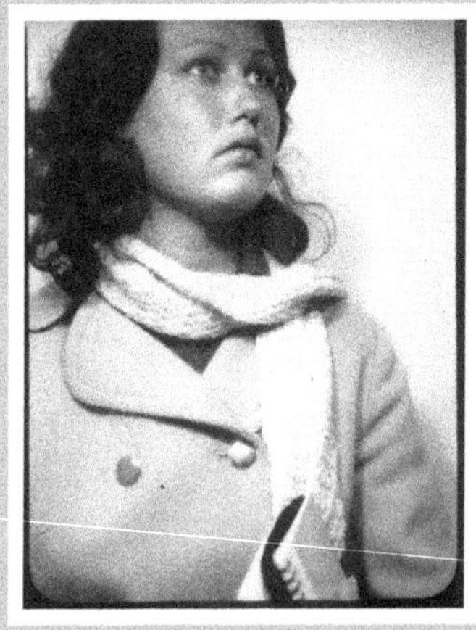
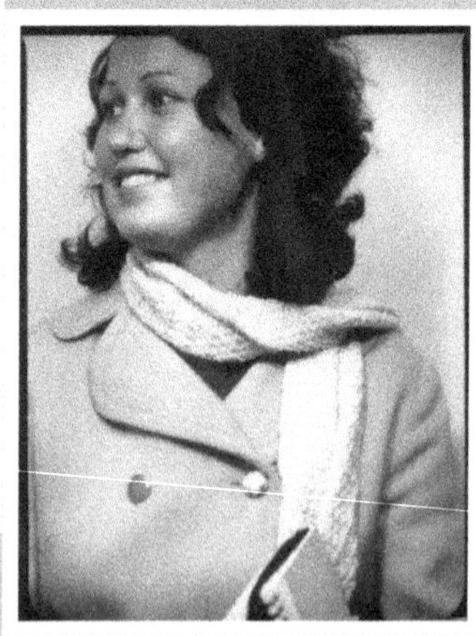
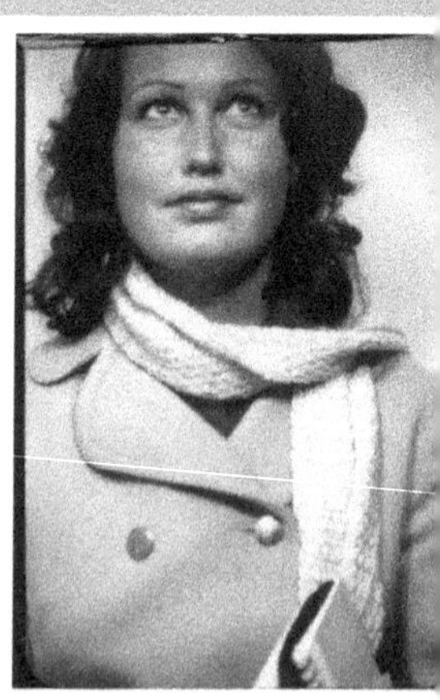
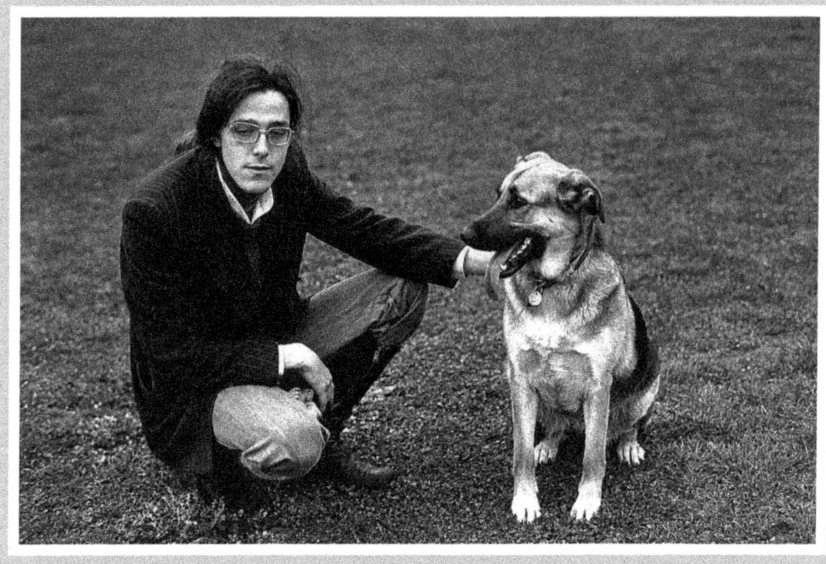

14

Destiny

Sometimes the world can be thought of as always changing, as something infinitely mutable, a flux, a foam. Not so much a thing, but an agent of change, a dynamo in an unimaginable machine.

Or it can be seen as implacable; obdurate and unyielding, perhaps even indifferent. A place not to be appeased. There are, seemingly, no concessions we can make or, if they can be made, the experience will empty us, and we will have no longer any sense of ourselves. It remains an implacable world.

Perhaps it is this that gives us the feeling that we do not belong here – that this is not a place for us; we, for whom amelioration, mitigation and compromise come, if not as second nature then at least third or fourth. Deracinated from some centre that may have once claimed us but is now all but forgotten.

Acceptance is always acceptance of the implacability of the world that inhabits us, even if we feel that we do not inhabit it.

The sky, the black branches of a winter tree, the hardwood floor below our feet, all this we yield to. 'Knowledge' is the word we give to our one-eyed appeasement; our bowing with ill-grace to the hard surface of the world that remains, in the face of all our 'knowing' utterly implausible.

I draw great comfort in being an animal, it helps to soften the brittle position that being in the world puts me in. Peculiar, but no exception; arranged in natural order, but then only to be singled out.

But then, I am no animal I recognise. And perhaps I am not recognised by any other animal in this pitiless place. And here, this place, perhaps this place is not recognisable as any place at all.

* * *

When I was a child, I used simple blocks of wood to make pretty much anything I wanted, arranging and re-arranging the milled blocks of wood. The small blocks were thrown over the fence into our yard by the builders next door. They were constructing a house from a plan, from detailed drawings: they knew precisely the end result of their endeavours.

My mother had asked the carpenters putting up the wooden frame to toss over any off-cuts for the use of her toddler. There seemed only to be a few kinds of block that came into our yard: rectangles (2" x 6"), square pieces (4" x 4") and, most valued, triangular pieces (6" x 2½").

Using my imagination and the properties of the blocks, I made many things; some had names, other constructions had no name but nevertheless played a role in the narrative which guided their use. These stories that governed this block city I have now forgotten.

Like my childhood dwelling place, the universe of the grown-ups is constructed out of a few simple building blocks. I had no names for the individual blocks of solid wood that I combined to make my world. The names for the simple building blocks for the wider universe have been invented to designate particles that are all but invisible.

This pen, this hand, me sitting here, the house around me, the cold winter sky, the planets circling the Sun, one of billions of stars in this slowly rotating spiral galaxy, one in a universe still expanding after 13.8 billion years, is all constructed from four building blocks. Two quarks and two leptons.

The up quark, the down quark, the electron (to do all the chemistry) and the electron neutrino. These four bits are all that is needed to build a universe. The mixing, combining, separating and cooking is governed by four fundamental forces which include gravity and electromagnetism. There are not many recipes that specify just four ingredients, and precisely name the whisks and oven temperature to be used.

And you and I are even simpler, we and all other living things are comprised of just three blocks, the two quarks and the electron; three invisible things, whose place in time and space is merely the sum of probabilities.

* * *

In the world of the Walrus and the Carpenter where we can walk upon the beach and talk of shoes and ships and sealing wax, we are enveloped by the is-ness of the world around us. The moment is just as it is, and not any other way.

It is only when suddenly something unexpected or terrible occurs that we consider that the moment could be otherwise, and we might not be tricked into becoming someone else's dinner. In fact some moments are so terrible we wish to undo a succession of moments, one after the other, going back in time. So far back that we might no longer be baby oysters with feet in shoes clean and neat; that the terrible absurdity of our current predicament be unstitched knit by purl.

This understanding that the moment could be other is the invocation of contingency, that other moments are possible but didn't occur for one reason or another; that this is-ness comes from a vast chain of occurrences linked by happenstance and was not preordained.

Contingency: if this, then that, and each this-and-that a function of decisions, choices, actions by us and the universe around us.

Though we have a Law of Gravity and rules governing the creation of the elements in nuclear fusion, there was no rule that required that our sun should come into existence some six billion year ago. But it did coalesce out of interstellar gas and from there a cascade of contingency resulted in this combination of quarks and electrons that is today able to write these words.

It is now time on our walk along the sand to speak of Fate, or Fates, for once there were three of them. The first spun the thread of life, another measured the thread out, and the third Fate chose the manner of death and cut the thread off. These are the three Greek Fates and, importantly, they were independent – both man and the gods had to submit to the good and bad moments predetermined by the unravelling thread controlled by the Fates.

These days the dictionary is somewhat vague, referring to an 'agency' or 'power' rather than the trio of ancient spinners. But the key thing is that our moments, all of them, marked out on the finite strand, are predetermined and as such are not part of an individual's life – agency in one's own life has been taken away. The moments are fixed, we just have to walk through them: as the oysters walk along the night shore of Lewis Carroll's terrible poem.

There can be no choice in a fated life – one's destiny (the actual living out of what has been preordained), rules out any exercise of choice. There is *nothing* contingent here: no possibility that the plump young oysters might heed the warnings of their elders. (Nor any chance that Lewis Carroll *did not* write his poem at all.)

* * *

These two photos are of two twenty-year-olds who happen to meet in their late thirties and stay together, then marry years later when they were in their mid-fifties. Retired now, the couple live in a small inland town. Both pursued professional careers in the capital city before moving out to the country. They have become members of the local community and have made new friends through local work and social groups.

They have a small vegetable patch where they grow tomatoes and herbs. They cultivate a few fruit trees including a fig tree which give them produce in the autumn. The woman has retired and the man still works part-time locally.

The photographs here are now over forty-five years old.

When this strip of photos was taken, the woman worked for a government department as a civil servant. Her office was in a building situated on a grand boulevard that travels from the city to the southern suburbs. It was originally an army barracks, and several cannons sit on the lawn, pointing their spiked barrels out across the tree-lined thoroughfare.

On the day of the photo the young woman used her lunch hour to take a tram into the city to get her picture taken at a photo booth. These booths once stood on street corners and were used to take basic black and white pictures at the cost of a few coins.

Once inside the curtained booth the young woman puts money into the slot and sits down. She pushes a button and the camera takes four quick photos.

Outside the booth she retrieves the strip from a slot in the side of the booth.

She is wearing a knee-length camel coloured double-breasted woollen coat with a loose knit white woollen scarf around her neck. She holds a folded note book. In it she is writing a letter to her partner who lives on the other side of the country. He has asked her to send him a picture of herself. Perhaps this is why the strip we see now only contains three images from an original set of four. The missing one she has sent to him with her letter.

She had recently visited him and he had not wanted her to go back east, but she only had her annual leave and had already paid for the return airline ticket.

She is not destined, years in the future, to meet the man she is now married to; the Greek spinners are long gone, so too the gods, there is just history now, the long line of happenstance. No thread connects this young woman getting her photo taken to the young man crouched down beside a dog in a park.

Just quarks and electrons linking atoms, making molecules, cells, and all heated by nuclear fusion, with entropy to point the way to a future time and place.

No necessity binds the two young people in these photos together; no predetermined chain compels the woman to meet the man with his hair tied back, there is nothing 'inevitable' here. There is no destiny they need to fulfil, just the unforseen casual links of contingency that give rise to the moment of their accidental meeting some years after the photos were taken. They were not meant to be.

The young man squats on the grass next to a Labrador-Alsation. Her tongue hangs out, panting, perhaps after a run across the park. Another cold day by the look of it. He wears something dark under his shirt then a jumper on top of that and finally a double-breasted pinstripe suit coat. He rests his hand on the back of the dog, who looks at him eye-to-eye. But the young man is not looking at anything; perhaps musing on some of the difficulties he is faced with in his current circumstances. The dog meanwhile is perhaps waiting for the young man to pick up the stout stick and run with it again.

In the photographs neither person is looking at anyone. They are not looking at us. Both wear a double-breasted coat. That's it.

At any point it may have been different. It is not random — contingency, one might say, is constrained. One cannot foretell the future and yet, when the future arrives, the experienced is–ness of the moment makes us want to say: 'it was meant to be', 'they have found each other', or, 'he is the one for her' or, more generally: 'everything happens for a reason'.

The vacuity of such a statement is maybe a little misleading. 'Everything happens for a reason' suggests all events are purposed and that the final outcome is the fulfilment of an originating purpose. This is a teleological explanation, the cause and the reason for a particular outcome is in its final purpose: the outcome we experience.

So rather than a trivially true statement that events are the result of chains of proximate causes (contingent events), 'it was meant to happen' becomes akin to an invocation of a fate, a foreordained destiny, in which the outcome is proof of its 'reasonableness' or, more strongly, the outcome is the result of necessity.

For those who evince such thinking these phrases may serve as antidotes to fears that a terrible randomness governs their life – a fear that no-one and nothing is in control, that nothing oversees the events and the consequences of their life. But if everything happens for a reason their life has a rationality within which they have a place, perhaps foreordained and necessary, but a place nevertheless.

There are laws that exist everywhere and for everyone but they are obscured by contingency and are indifferent to anything we might care about. These laws and scientific theories are reasoned but do not generate a narrative, but merely specify the quarks and leptons required to make a universe and, in this particular universe, specify the building blocks that make living things who can make stories up in the yard as they play.

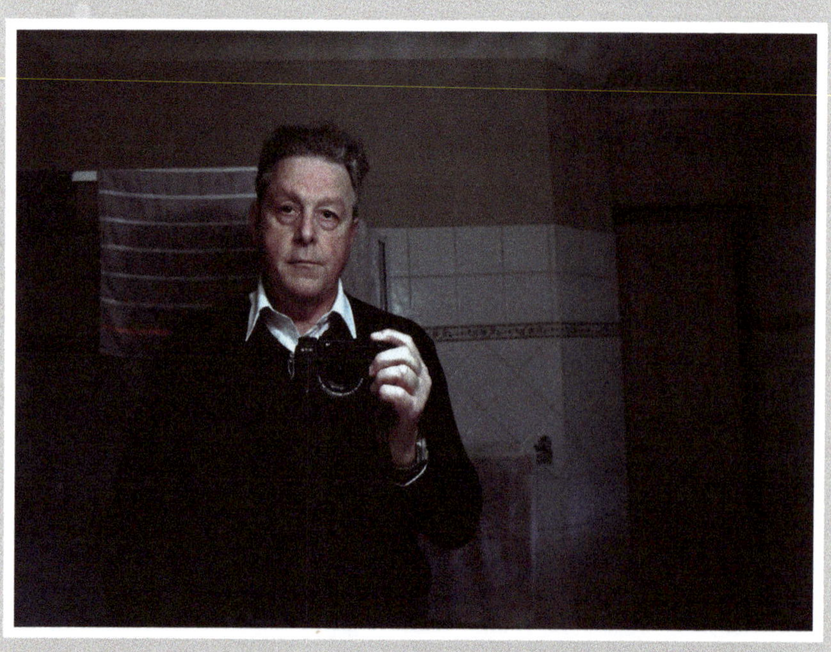

15

Self-Portrait

A picture taken to check on our own presence: that there is a face of oneself. The constant experience of being in another's gaze, a slow rubbing away of the features, seen, and seen again, not reanimating but being wiped away as if with a damp cloth. Clearing the expressions of all expression, so that it becomes a template for some other's fear or frustration, or a blank for the signs of someone else's love and recognition.

The terrible otherness, that once ingested, begins to reform one's own cells in the likeness of somebody else. A face in the service of another person looking out; someone else capturing the cold sky, the scent of green, the shadows that move across a stone wall and, higher up, the sway of pines on a ridge. All this, so vivid, so absolutely true but, of course, just what someone else sees – having meaning for them, to be sure, but for us some postcard picture placed in the wrong letter box.

So, the capture of oneself in a mirror, reversed, mediated, conspired for – perhaps not even a capture but proof of life for whoever holds us at bay. A moment of re-positioning, thinking maybe of a gesture truly recognisable. A pose to convince those with the power over life and death – something to counter, if only fleetingly, the usurper's picture – a real presence. A face that they will begin with, maybe the first of tradable counters in a game of quantities.

So, the self-portrait when there is no one to watch, to take what verisimilitude can be mustered for the occasion, when identity becomes a matter for conjecture. A face for the other, briefly re-purposed. But for what purpose? This question is not really answerable; the face in the mirror asks – are you then the hostage taker? The house is empty – no-one will know that I am inside, or know that it is even me – the one to re-purpose this face for my own ends.

Is the picture of the mask that, necessarily, I must inhabit for the sake of everyone around me? So that I can be seen and passed by; or loved by those who recall some feeling they once had, when this face did not look like it does now but the wearer is intuited and consistencies are noticed even as the sun passes overhead and when winter supplants autumn?

The photographed face constitutes quite an arbitrary relationship, like a word and its referent, we force connections before we know there can be no connection. The beginning of a foisted causality within the world of our parents and teachers. Those who purpose us for the day, those for whom we learn the art of correlation, and whose subsequent recognition of the other confirms the fate of all faces.

Not really knowing the face in the mirror, we concentrate on the background, consider the mix of horizontals and verticals, a frame within a frame, the sheen of the bathroom mirror 'discoloured' by soap and dust and water vapour.

'What is that fellow looking at?' we ask ourselves, smiling to camouflage the anger at not having an answer. At being somehow caught out doing the unthinkable: looking at nothing at all. Trying to compose a picture with the accidents of geometry and light, knowing the vacuum at the centre of it will be what holds people's attention – it is what they are there for.

Still, the house is empty and the capture is all your own, even if, purely illusory, just a function of a photograph you have not been able to refrain from taking.

* * *

I showed a friend of mine a picture of me and someone else, standing together in a park. I spent a moment, perhaps too many moments, explaining over our coffee and cake, who this other person was, a person whom my morning-tea friend had never met.

He sat next to me in the little cafe and pointed his finger at the photograph and asked: 'But who is *this* guy?' He was impatient as if something was being withheld from him. He was pointing at the other figure in the picture – at me, his friend, sitting next to him showing him this picture.

'That's me', I say without thinking.

'Oh – the people look hard; why the down-turned mouths?' And now that I *was* thinking I found I had nothing to say.

'It looks like a picture from the eighteenth century. A time full of stern looking characters.' My friend laughs now, having recovered himself, so to speak.

The person my friend had not recognised is the same person in the mirror taking his own picture. We may wonder if it is the self-portraitist who is now asking: 'who is this guy?', impatiently, as if, again, something is being held back from him: a necessary ingredient which, when withheld, prevents any true recognition.

In the café I had somehow put everyone in a false position, no one was really being recognised here, we were all put beyond knowing anything about ourselves, let alone one another.

But in a minute we put away the picture of complete strangers and closed the box. This would not disrupt our regular morning tea together; any embarrassment was soon dispersed by the opening of the cafe door, the buttoning up of overcoats against the cold outside.

Still, the people in the photograph and those who had just viewed them were all, now, in some way unknown and, if truth be told, a little repudiated; they were no longer what they seemed an hour ago. A taking away from, or a layering had now occluded the original image and had done so for good. There could be no undoing the question of 'who is this guy?'

* * *

It would seem that when we look into the face of another, there is always someone else we are looking out for. Every face is a proxy, something that is standing in for the face we really wish to see – to come face to face with, if you like.

A tacit assumption is that the face we are trying to see through, the face we are looking at, is another face altogether, but still one that belongs to the person who stands in front of us. This assumption we do not care to examine closely, for the idea that in piercing the cover of the face we may discover someone else entirely is too frightening. So we entertain our suspicions, but only so far: for a known face, a recognised person, to be suddenly someone completely different would undermine not just the person involved but the whole notion of recognition.

A parent's face we know from the outset is not that of our mother or father but of some entity we are only too glad to have a face for – a face that we can learn to believe in, knowing that behind it is a place where, despite ourselves, everything is unmoored, a place that shows us we are all at sea.

The loved one's face is searched out, but because of our affections there is no chance that our penetrating enquiry will reveal another face – until of course we fall out of love and withhold the special dispensation we have hitherto accorded this lost love to have been someone else with impunity.

A self-portrait is merely an instance of this looking, but perhaps we make exceptions with ourselves. We know from being, in some sense, inside the face that we are something completely unlike the image we can see on the page or that others may recognise in daily life. So, we *know* the falsity of the face we take the photograph of, we know it presents necessarily something other, there can be no deception for us, even if we realise we can never undeceive the person, anyone who, on the outside, attempts to look in.

In that sense we are resigned to never being seen. It is only the recognition of us by those who, through long association, have quelled their suspicions that we are someone completely other. That we *present another person* if only their fond glances were perspicacious enough to discern the true features beneath those worn thin with their attention.

So, when family or friends say they do not like the picture I have taken, my curiosity is only partially feigned. 'Why?' I ask, 'What's wrong with it?'

'Well', they explain and point to blotchy skin or eyebrows or the lines around the eyes. The disconnect is quite profound – they think that I look like this. On what occasion is it that a word looks like its referent?

I may be being a little hard, those who know me have more invested, as it were, in not giving way to their suspicions concerning the true face they are, for my sake, trying not to discern behind my features, but know is there.

✳ ✳ ✳

Arthur Rimbaud was famous for saying once 'Je est un autre'. The phrase is in a letter to friend and translates as 'I is another'. He gave up being a poet in Paris at the age of twenty-one and went out to Africa.

He left poetry and what his practice revealed to him, for another life in another place. He knew wherever he was, whatever he did (poetry, soldiery, gun running, trading in slaves, or coffee) he was always an other. This was a great freedom, he could be at sea with impunity.

There is a self-portrait: he stands on grass with the trunk of a tree beside him, behind there are palm fronds, and a shrub with berries. He wears white trousers and white jacket. He sports a moustache with upward pointing waxed tips and a tight cap on his head. He seems relaxed, his left leg forward and his weight on his right leg, torso tilting back just a little. But his arms are crossed and his expression is stern as he looks at 'un autre' behind the camera. It is dated 1883, Harar, Ethiopia.

16

The Missing Photograph

The photographs you have are in a box or an album, on your phone, a USB stick or a PC, they don't count; they've never been counted, they are innumerable. They are not the ones you want, the one you want is singular – it is the one that is missing.

I have been looking for it, this missing photograph the one I just can't seem to locate. Though there is a doubt that I am looking hard enough. I mean I search when, for some reason or other, I feel myself to be at a loss. Perhaps when the day has been cold and I have gone out up the two steps into the wintry back yard where the sun comes brightly. It comes filtered through a filigree of black sticks that wave when the breeze strikes the elm branches hard enough. On days like that, like a reckless reptile, I stand face up, eyes closed, lost to all good sense, wishing only to be warmed for a moment; perhaps so that once again I can think again of what it is I have to find.

So, here I am in front of an old box of black and white prints, flicking through, turning over, putting them right way up, pausing, remembering, not recalling at all – of course I am, but moving quickly, looking for something that is not there. Do any of these come close? Close to what?

Is it an ur-photograph? Something that came before all the others?

Like that view of a Parisian street. The photographer is high up, perhaps looking out a loft window down on the bustling street.

The photograph shows us the wide cobbled roadway, full of carts and horses, passing along between pavements where further back, stand a row of buildings which range in height from a single *étage* to five storeys high.

A bright day, for the awnings are pulled down over the pedestrians pausing to look into the shop windows. On the opposite pavement there are two rows of leafy trees and set among them are tall gaslights. The wide boulevard disappears towards the horizon as the sky bleaches white in this panoramic photograph.

The picture was taken in 1838 by Louis Daguerre and is often thought to be the first photographic image of a person. Because in the image there is only one clearly visible person. He stands with his left foot raised resting on a box. He is having his shoes polished. The shoe shiner is indistinct, so much so that some viewers have suggested that the man with his leg raised is standing in front of a public water pump.

The man and the shoe shiner are the only signs of life on this bright sunny morning in the Boulevard du Temple, a busy thoroughfare, famous at the time for its theatres, cafes and shopping.

All the life in this street has been erased by the photograph. Daguerre's Daguerreotype image required a seven minute exposure time that, while recording forever the still man having his left shoe shined, erases all the movement, all the shoppers, *flâneurs*, horses and carts, all the bustling busy life on the street and pavements of this cityscape.

If it is movement that characterises life then it is only the man's lack of liveliness, his immobility, his *lifelessness* that allows him to be immortalised here as the first person to be photographed. With the lens open all life around him has vanished, never to be recalled on this day on this street in Paris in 1838.

* * *

I'll know the missing picture when I see it, of course I will. I understand that I've not seen it yet, in fact, have never seen it (otherwise how could it be in anyway lost, irrevocably or otherwise?), which as you may imagine gives some urgency to the search.

Compounding all this, is that while the picture has always been missing, it was sometime before I became aware of this – up until quite recently I had no inkling of the need to find it. And a lot of time had been lost. And I understand the constraints that time now imposes on me: the time was not infinite in the first place. Also time's contractures and expansions are a law unto itself, our sense of time is just that and, like other senses, can be tricked, made ill, fail to operate or become subject to convincing illusion. There is trompe du temps to match the *trompe l'oeil*.

I drift from my point, I lapse from my search, I start one thing and finish another: the loose ends, middles without heads or tails, participles without subject, all have to be swept up at the end of the day, if for no other reason that only then can another day begin.

There are fears, variously clothed, that when it comes to it, I won't recognise the missing image for what it is. Costumed like a flight attendant, one fear announces that the plane will never land at all. The brace is all there is, and will last for eternity. Dressed as a barista who is mouthing over the sound of coffee grinding, making out with gestures and the bobbing of a full beard that the coffee will never be ground and that no *latte* is possible while the beans continue to turn to fine powder between the blades of the grinder.

Sometimes this fear is that I will not recognise the image I finally have in my hand or on the screen, that I will pass over it, not seeing that this is what has been missing all along, and sometimes this fear is all dressed up to look like me.

Shocking to tell, the impersonation is at first very convincing – I never fail to start with a racing heart, then clammy hands and shallow breathing. But panic is staved off when I spot the sly giveaways that tell me that this fear is not something of my own creation: the colour of the socks, the hat that is a knock-off, not my fedora from Fagolin of Udine, and the jumper – not a style I would ever wear.

My relief is great at this moment. These fears, once exposed as charlatans, imposters and cheap piecework, soon evaporate and I am left with some renewed certainty that soon I will find this image, the one above all others that needs to be found.

I have to be honest here. There is some possibility that a worse fate awaits not just the to-be-discovered image, but also me who will be the eventual discoverer of the image. I now must consider the possibility that I may indeed find the photo, have it firmly in my hands, recognise it for what it is and yet have no sense of completeness, no great and sustaining satisfaction, find that the meaning has all but drained away, that the image is merely a remnant and has power only to suggest what both it and I have lost. That we view one another as very old lovers whose affection in mutual recognition is only that, and that knowledge of shared memories has replaced the memories themselves.

For both of us meaning has leached away. And it has done so unbeknownst to both – the photograph could be an image of almost anything at all and I, looking on, could now be anyone at all. Both of us now merely generic at best and, at worst, unrecognisable by anyone at all. Invisible in a box of photos, invisible in the street full of shoppers, coffee drinkers and theatre goers.

* * *

Having considered all this, it may be possible just to imagine what the photograph that must exist contains. Or even better, not even imagine but relate the actual contents of the image as it appears on the photographic paper. This, I know, is a feat, the exercise of which, in the end, I may not be capable. Still, today, I feel it must be tried.

The image is that of a landscape seen through open French doors. The wooden doors fold back against the white wall on one side, and press against drawn curtains on the other. A white wooden slat balustrade runs across the open doorway and separates the inside and the outside. The photograph appears to have been taken from the second storey and looks down along the boundary fence and the tropical bush that separates two gleaming white five-storey apartment buildings.

I look down through the slats that prevent one from falling out and onto the paved yard ten feet below. I can make out several species of ferns growing thick out of a dry rocky soil. Higher up are narrow-leafed tea-green shrubs and small trees with shiny yellow and sea-green variegated leaves.

All this creates a narrow corridor of impenetrable foliage stretching back between the converging building walls. Growing as straight as the walls and window shutters are the palm trees, some narrow others thicker with coconuts bunched yellow beneath the careless cascade of fronds. Then, towering over all the palms and gabled roofs are the creamy, paper-swathed boughs of the great melaleucas reaching out over the tops of buildings and palms alike.

The strong tropical light casts shadows of the living trees onto the walls, the balconies and narrow eaves of the apartment walls, bringing to them a form of life; their once monolithic shapes now constantly moving, shifting in a play of dark and light that animates and joins them to the other living things, breathing and moving with purpose.

* * *

Have I convinced you? Has my ekphrasis brought something vividly to your imagination's eye? For it is only conviction that can bring the missing photograph from its mystery. For itself, the unimagined image is content – it has no necessity to reveal itself. There is a compulsion for it to be viewed; but it is only we who suffer compulsions, encourage necessity, and mollify fears.

The image is an empty page but not to us.

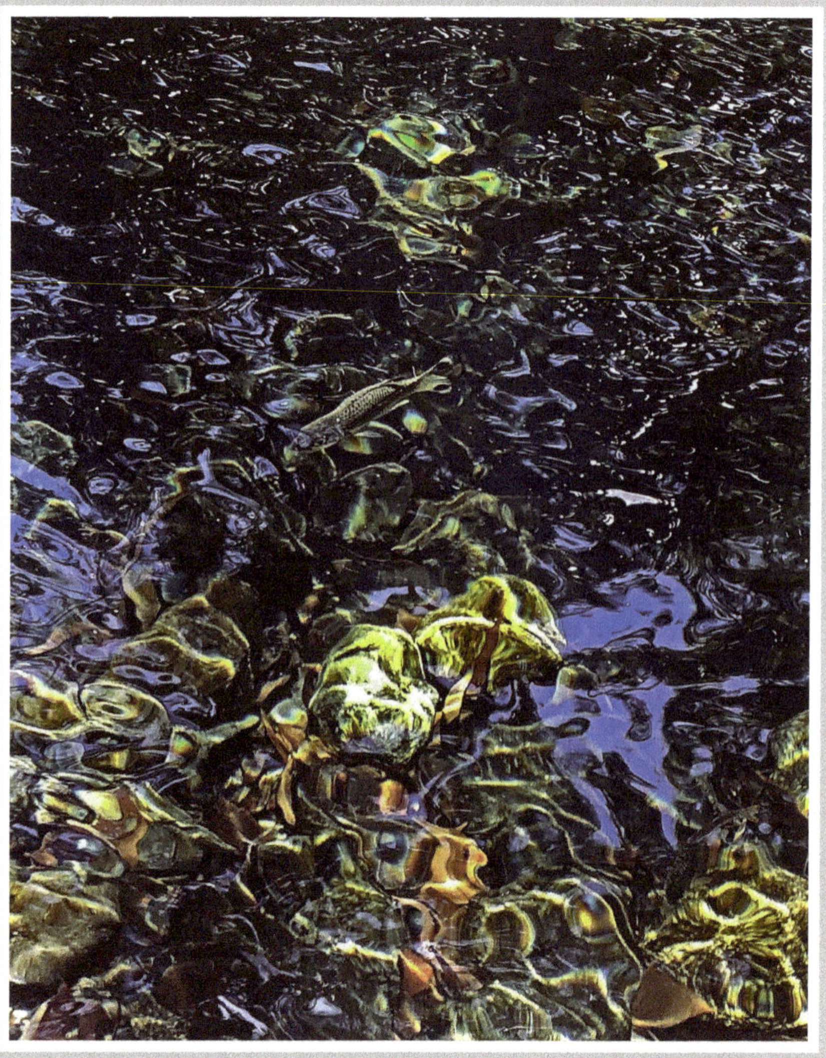

17

The Creek

After I took this picture we turned back. It was mid-afternoon and we had come as far as we were able. This was the end of the tour, the end of the road. The forest went on and there was a four-wheel drive track that others could take.

Our guide was laying out tropical fruit on a trestle table erected on flat stony ground a few metres from the sandy creek edge. He wanted us all to try the custard apple, banana, papaya and black sepote.

We had all come a long way to this creek in the rainforest. None of us had been here before. A family from Spain, two English friends with a regional accent that our host mistook for another language. A couple from Naples, a solo traveller from Oregon, and a smattering of Australians.

Our guide laid out black skinned fruit, knobbly skinned fruit, and a species of banana with seed not sold in supermarkets. He enjoyed his work, he drove the bus, cooked the lunch, poured tea and told us of Cook's misadventures out on the Great Barrier Reef. Our guide said he enjoyed meeting interesting people, that he was semi-retired and took these full-day safaris only once or twice a week.

He knew a lot about the flora of the rainforest, but did not tell us much about himself. He said he was an introvert and struggled to make himself interesting to others.

He wanted to include us in his enjoyment. He knew what the forest could be used for, he trained as a botanist and was not from around here. Soon he would be gone, he told us, and would miss doing these tours. He enjoyed meeting interesting people.

Soon he would join his wife who was taking up a new position in Victoria, a place at the other end of the country, some 2,500 kilometres to the south, near from where we had come to make this trip to the wet tropics in Queensland.

When I took this picture of the riffling water, the tour had been travelling north since the early morning and now, in mid-afternoon, we had all seen many things, walked in the forest and been out on the water in a wide-hulled, shallow draught boat.

We were a quiet lot, our host wished we would all get on, be interesting to one another, but we did not speak much. Perhaps our silence was in response to the enfolding quiet of the forest; the great hoop pines disappearing into the clear sky hundreds of metres above; there was little sound from the vine-crowded trees along the river banks or from the sun-broken canopy tilting high over our heads. There was no one speaking to us from the undergrowth, full of pale shadows and small flowers, sprays of glossy green leaves and bright blue fleshy nuts lying like globes of bright sky amongst the dark leaf litter.

We had been picked up in the purpose-built bus from our hotels, apartments, and resorts, the beaches to the north on the coast, places where we visitors all came to stay. We travelled to escape our local winter or fulfil a wish to see a special place, or perhaps just tick off an item on a bucket list.

It was an ancient rainforest. Where we walked in silence was a remnant of a vast forest that had existed for hundreds of millions of years as it floated over the globe on Gondwana. As recently as 15 million years ago this forest covered the interior of the island continent, but now what remained hugged the coast above the Tropic of Capricorn from Townsville to Cooktown.

To get into the World Heritage listed Daintree National Park we need to cross the wide tidal Daintree River. The most common route in is by ferry; a big car-carrying platform drawn across the water by cables pulled by motors on either side of the river.

But today our tour group goes across the water by boat. The man at the tiller takes us on a route between an island and the southern bank. Mangroves, mud, the dark green water, and the wall of forest dotted with tall trees providing detail against the featureless blue sky above. In the distance a blue mountain peak lifts the horizon briefly.

The boatman cuts the engine and into the sudden quiet the forest presses closer; we glide between the mangrove roots piercing up out of the shiny mud. We pay attention to what passes by in a faint hiss of insect calls. We pay attention to the forest that pays us none.

It is just the estuarine crocodiles coming to life on the sunlit mudflats that scent and count us one by one.

* * *

The bus stops at a roadhouse for lunch. Our guide, Bob, fires up the barbeque as we wander inside the wooden cafe for water or coffee. Back outside we find benches and a long table under cover and sit down.

Bob is throwing steaks and sausages on the hot plate. There are cold salads in big plastic containers. Some travellers have gone off to pet wallabies. I ask Bob if he wants some help in preparing lunch for all sixteen of us. 'No, no', he says happily, turning onions and rolling sausages. I persist: 'It's a long day and you're doing everything.' 'I love doing this', Bob says without stopping, 'I enjoy meeting interesting people.'

I am hungry and can smell the meat cooking. I sense that this is Bob's way of getting away from us all, of keeping busy, keeping us at bay, the difficulties of talking with 'interesting people'. I don't think one becomes a botanist because one loves interacting with people. In among the strangler vines, the giant melaleucas and figs, explaining the uses of palm fronds, the distribution of seeds by cassowaries, pointing out five-hundred year old cycads and the yellow upright caterpillars mimicking poisonous prey, our host has a role, a purpose in being among humans who are always calling out, continually addressing everyone they see; incessantly demanding accountability, a reply. They can do little else.

I sit with other travellers at the table away from the barbeque. The woman opposite tells me she has travelled to all the continents, climbed most mountain ranges and is now doing the tropics, here and in Borneo. She is from Oregon and describes the town near the Idaho border where she lives and works. She pauses and looks at me: "You probably think that we're all crazy."

"Absolutely", I say, looking straight back at her. She then asks me where I'm from. That is all we say about all her country men and women who voted for the current president of the United States. "I'm from Central Victoria", I say and try to give her bearings, so she knows roughly where I've travelled from to get here.

* * *

Back on the bus we head north again. To our west, the bush continues across the peninsula to the shores of the Gulf of Carpentaria and, to the east, the forest tumbles down to the shore of the Coral Sea. We are travelling north to Cape Tribulation and beyond until we can go no further.

We pass lodges, eco-rentals, ice-creameries, teahouses, meditation and yoga camps, fishing, surfing and mangrove tours, adventure camps, spas and farm stays. Soon even these barely glimpsed hideaways and their signs give way to the forest. Our track, once sealed, soon turns to dust. Out the windows the thick wide leaves of roadside bush become a uniform pale grey. It is the dry and the dirt, beaten with tyres, turns to a fine spray that coats whatever is close to hand.

This is a four-wheel-drive track only and we see few other vehicles on the corrugated path. This is just as well as the sharp turns are all blind, and the track is barely wide enough to accommodate passing cars and buses.

Bob is telling us, amongst the gear changes, accelerations and braking, that we are going to a creek where we all can have a swim in clear running water.

There he will feed us tropical fruit and brew tea for us to drink. So the bus shudders on, twisting up, and coiling down the narrow corridor that the bush has been parted to create, and then, only temporarily, for it closes its dusty foliage quickly behind us.

My eyes have to re-adjust suddenly to the open vista we now seemed to have stumbled into. In fact it is just widening of the road into a car parking area. I see trees, campers, and high-axled 4WDs. There are a few people standing around, they seemed at a loss, they didn't seem to be looking at anything, and move purposelessly in the clearing that soon leads away down to the unseen murmuring running creek.

Suddenly I am aware that our host is asking for help. Out of the back of the bus he is pulling folded tables that he is asking us to carry, "only a little way", he says, pointing vaguely.

By the bright dancing glaze of transparent water we all stand still. Despite our host's excited gestures no one seems to have the slightest interest in going for a swim in the creek. We stand looking around us, occasionally venturing a little way down amongst the polished stones onto the fine sand edge of the pool where the flashing surface seems to move like molten glass, enlarging and colouring what lies shallow in its cooling heart.

No-one wanted to speak, we seemed to drift away from our fellow travellers, finding enough space so the thick-vined banks, and the lightly rippling stream of sounding light might capture us completely, hold us adrift from all that might address us – when all we wanted was for the stream to briefly undo us, leave us nameless.

No-one swims, at most we take off our shoes and stand ankle deep, eyes downward watching the small, speckled jungle trout swim around us, sharp and sleek, swimming inches above the rippling stones, leaves and fine yellow sand of the creek bed.

Our host wants to serve us exotic fruit but there would be time for that later. We look upstream into the sun, and downstream where the forest and creek run together towards the glittering horizon. We would taste the fruit later but not now.

An official description I read later about this spot carries an enticement of sorts, saying: "there are few other safe places to swim in the Daintree lowlands." There is also a warning as well, that: "... it is not wise to travel any further north."

We all knew this was a place that we could only turn back from: this water was a beginning and an end.

18

Three Images Remembered

The house in which my siblings and I grew up was always called '56' after the number of the house in the street in which it stood. I was about ten when we moved into the solid brick Victorian house.

The house had ducted heating fuelled by oil stored in a large square tank. It was raised high off the ground on square metal legs and bolted to the side of the external wall. Hot air was pushed around the house coming up through louvred vents that could be opened and closed. These adjustable oblong metal frames were screwed over the neat holes cut in the Baltic pine floors throughout the house.

The furnace that burnt the oil to generate the warm air was in a small room off the main hallway. It was a big box that took up most of the space in this windowless room that we called the heater room. The rest of the space was taken up with shelves stacked with towels and blankets, and bed linen, which was always warm.

My grandfather would often come to stay with us over the years of my childhood. Why he stayed with us I never knew; he was a quiet and solitary man. He wasn't with us now and boxes of his books were stored on the floor beneath the stacked shelves of the heater room.

One day my mother and I were looking through some of her father's boxes. She was wondering what to do with them. One cardboard box was full of identically bound volumes. I remember picking up one of the heavy grey volumes to see what they had in them. These were very heavy big books and I struggled to open the pages which were thick and textured, they were creamy yellow, and filled with columns of dark print.

The image I came upon was small plate of a World War I battleship being raised out of the ocean years after the war had ended. The black and white photograph was rich with tones of grey ranging from ice grey to a warm brown and provided startling detail of the enormous ship, prow-first, jutting out of the waves, many metres tall against the white sky.

I was stunned by the image. This was a great and powerful object being pulled up from the bottom of the ocean. It was strangely draped in seaweed, thick grey gleaming stuff from places which are never seen, that only exist invisibly, covered by the waves of vast oceans. But now I could see details of the metal prow beneath the strange, long, flat, clinging weed. An anchor was still firmly set in the side of the once powerful battleship. I could see the railing, still intact, running in a V shape around the pointed prow of the ship.

I was shocked that this image could exist. All of this, the sunken ship, the seaweed and the barnacles that marred the once sleek side, none of this should ever be seen. It had been dragged off the bottom of the ocean, a realm that belonged only to the imagination.

That this image existed could only mean that the natural and absolute order had been tampered with. Something was being shown here that should never be seen. There was a horror that something so irrevocably lost should, many years later, suddenly re-appear. The bow reared up vertically as it never could have when it was a mighty ship of the navy. In piercing the waves and sky it was revealing something that could only appal, it had become something against nature.

The book became heavy, and many times I re-arranged it in my cradling arms as they grew achy-tired in their work of holding it up.

I didn't think of the destruction of this ship in war, nor consider the deaths of sailors as the ship sank to the bottom of the sea. It was more that, once vanquished, the boat had no business coming back to life; to resurface was something supernatural, something truly shocking and confounding.

* * *

A few years later I had my own room. It was a very small room that was at the end of a short corridor that ran from the kitchen to what, for some reason, was called 'the maid's room'. The only other room off this corridor was the pantry full of dry goods, tinned food and whatever else couldn't be stored in the small kitchen.

A small room, but mine, away from my younger siblings. It had a single bed and above the bed head, bracketed to the wall, was a small shelf upon which was an old valve-filled radio. On the opposite wall was another shelf desk-high where I kept my school books and exercise books. My window looked out across the fence onto the brick wall of a two storey private hotel.

At that age I had not much use for newspapers though I remember once having a geography project that required I cut out the small black and white weather maps that the morning newspaper published daily. I pasted these small maps into my exercise book. Otherwise I would only glance at the headlines of 'The Herald' or the morning 'The Age' as I collected it from the box at the driveway entrance.

But I did cut out a photograph that appeared in one of these newspapers. It was a photograph that took up most of the front page on the day it was published. A grainy black and white image of a man falling high in the sky. He had fallen from the wheel well of a commercial airliner just after takeoff.

The image had been blown up so that there was little detail, but the falling body was clear against the uniform light grey sky. The man was falling backwards into the air, through the empty sky, and his body and limbs were all in positions they would never adopt if he were safely on the ground. The man's legs were in such a way they could never support his body weight, and his arms, bent at the elbow and slightly raised, were not in a position that they could carry anything. The tilt of his torso, the raised legs and bent arms, a configuration that was only possible if the man was weightless; the body in an arrangement where it had absolutely no work to do.

I cut the picture out of the newspaper and stuck it up on my wall above the radio, stuck it to the painted plaster wall with cellotape.

It was not an image to think about; I did not find out how this picture came about, or who this falling man was. The grainy picture, that captured by accident this free fall, was absolute in its way. It required no story, no adumbration. I don't know if anyone else saw the rough newspaper cutting on my wall, I don't remember talking to anyone about it. What could be said?

It was an impossible position.

* * *

The two volume *Colour Atlas of Pathology* had many pictures. So many pictures that, with subsequent viewings, I never recall seeing the same picture twice. They were heavy volumes; the pages impregnated with chalk, with colour plates on every page. If I were bored I would take down a volume for a quick look at the pictures illustrating parts of people and the diseases that disfigured them. I couldn't take much, so they were fleeting glances, then, perhaps a quick flick to some other page. Not looking, not even really wishing to see, but avidly turning pages for something else, worse, better.

In my mind I now wander through the rooms of this house of fifty years ago, I am looking for the bookshelf in which these grey and red bound volumes sat always together. There were books everywhere in 56, our kids' books in shelves standing or attached to walls in the bedrooms, and then parents' books in the living rooms. I look everywhere now but can only see the gold lettering on the spine; unable to see the room nor the shelf where the two always stood.

They were my father's books, prescribed textbooks from when he was studying medicine at the university.

And I was twelve or thirteen and bored and restless, nothing held my attention, there was nothing that I wanted to attend to; skip on the shining wooden floors, pull the light cord for that satisfying click when the switch in the high ceiling turned the lights on or off. It didn't matter, just the desire to move from one state to another, and again.

It was then I might pull down one of these horrible and fascinating books. The images were disgusting: faces of people covered in red spots or worse. Page after colour page, swollen arms, gangrenous legs, more faces distended by tumours and disfigured by lesions, open wounds, infections full of disgusting stuff.

The revulsion would build quickly until the book was snapped shut, it made a terrible noise all these heavy pages coming together; strong, shiny binding holding the colour plates full of disease and deformity fast, and all the edges forming a seamless solid wall of paper.

But the revulsion is what drew me there. Something that dispelled all boredom, held the attention in a grip that, only with difficulty, could be shaken free. And afterwards forgotten completely.

I'd climb the fence, use the fruit tree to clamber onto the low tin roof of the wooden room at the back of the red brick house. Up then onto the slate roof, climbing carefully, the balls of my feet resting briefly where the tacks held the slippery grey slate to the wooden frame. Up to the top, sit astride the pitched roof capped in tin. Look out over the houses, the tops of elms and oaks, telegraph poles and the distant hazy mountains to the east.

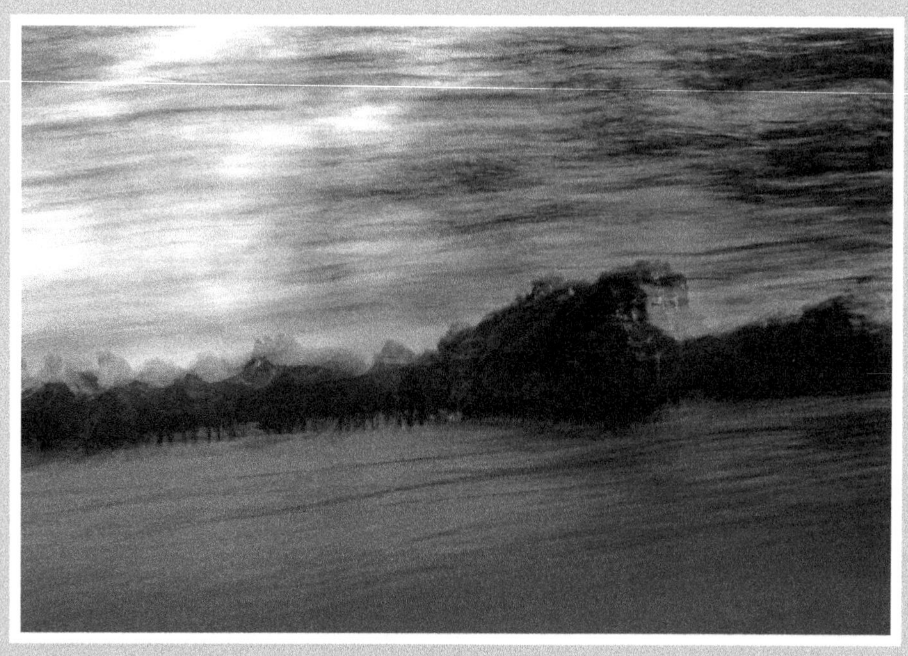

19

Landscape

These are trees in a paddock. Sometimes I look and think the trees are marching towards me; the ones at the front racing towards me beginning to tower over me as the perspective distorts with their rapid approach.

But mostly I have no idea of what I'm looking at when I glance up at this image on the white pinboard. It makes me a little uneasy; I probably know exactly what I'm seeing but don't have the words.

A line of trees at the back of a paddock. A streaky sky, blue and white with wavy black marks all brushed, it seems, from left to right. The sky darkens above the tight copse of trees that angles out, breaking the line of the horizon. I can't help but think of Birnam Wood coming closer, very quickly.

But on the day when I looked out the car window I never saw any of this: it's a landscape created by the internal workings of the camera. It is a landscape only by convenience. In fact, let's say this is not a landscape, but something invented, an accident, a *mechanism*. Not something ever seen, but a construction out of metal, an engine, and carefully cut glass. I never saw this, just as Macbeth did not believe in the possibility of the wood's movement against him.

That Sunday I sat in the front passenger seat looking out through the side window. Our journey home began in a forest. Shafts of vertical light alternate with the black pillars of straight messmate and ash. The canopy flashes overhead in green and grey, shadows stop and start in cobalt blue and chalkboard black and, beneath, the white scribbles of sudden forest clearings.

We are coming home from a visit to a private garden and nursery open to the public. The grounds had been cut from the thick bush in mountainous country. We went for a walk around the well-tended and labelled beds. Later we bought seeds to sew and bulbs to plant in our garden at home.

Once out of the forest, the day grew grey as low cloud seemed to seep up out of the low hills and shallow gullies running through open pasture. The road was flat but spotted with several cars ahead of us, and some other cars coming towards us; we listened to the AFL match on the radio.

And out of the camera comes this picture slightly sinister in its blur; dark patches smeared across the clouds but not part of any sky I know. On the horizon trees ghost trees, all linked solid green above the spindly trunks bent and walking in a tight formation towards us, rushing by in the car to outrun them, we hope.

Somewhere else the football strikes the post bringing a point and not another goal; a crowd of voices pitching out of the stands when the umpire blows the whistle. Is it our team who is being penalised for tackling too high?

I have the camera up to my eye, bracing it against the bumps and swerves of the road. I wedge my elbow in the right angle of the window frame and fire the shutter at what passes so quickly in front of the cold glass lens. I don't know what I'm looking for out the window; the grassed acres, lines of pine and gum marking the boundaries of paddocks, allotments, properties and invisible gullies and the occasional lines of white posts and rails for the horse studs.

Not a clue of what I'm looking for; perhaps nothing at all, just the sensation of motion, the fall of patchy sun on my eyelids, warming my blood for the moment, the slight roll of the car side to side on the uneven asphalt. The football commentary, murmured, indistinct yet constant, some reminder of another story teller.

There is none of this in the picture: startlement perhaps, the viewer or viewed. The captured moment still fleeting, still wanting not to be taken out of time, be cut from the completeness of the day: the sun, the sound of the radio, the seconds unbidden, unbroken.

Still, the trees in the paddock rushing towards us: something insistent, something wishing to assert an image that was not just manufactured, but living outside crafted glass and electronics. Not quite quick enough to catch as we go by at 100 kilometres an hour.

* * *

I know what this image is. But I have nothing but excuses for the reader. My disingenuousness knows no bounds. I will tell what I know about this artefact, this misdescription of what lay out through my passenger side window on a drive in the country one day in Autumn.

A distant line of trees in a paddock. Trees hunched at the edge of a featureless foreground. The trees pitch forward, the dry grass streaks to the right. Thickly leafed gums blur in motion but they are really just doubled, the shutter has recorded them twice. The reflected light has registered on the sensor for an eighth of a second and in that time the car has moved down the road, but relative to us the trees are now at a different position. By my calculations the car during that brief 1/8 second has moved 3.5 metres down the road. The trees have lurched after us as we pass and race away at 28 metres a second.

* * *

I remember vividly the day in art class when I first 'got' a Fred Williams' landscape. The class had been looking at slides of

Australian painters, the clicking carousel had thrown up several of Williams' paintings some of which I had seen before. But that morning, for some reason, I suddenly saw the one that flashed up on the screen. It was not a moment of interpretation but the sudden seeing of the bush, the trees, upright and fallen, the light bright, sharply coloured, and the dirt beneath it all. But more, the sudden opening out of space, the expanding distances, the stark structure of the countryside and its dense covering – a double image of skeleton and flesh.

Williams' painting depicted the whole landscape – it was not a notation or an abstraction; it was as lush and as detailed as a Glover or a von Guérard.

Now, in some way, when I see my local bush landscape, I see Fred Williams' picture of it; the local sclerophyll forests have been doubled. Neither one is obvious, neither one is occult. When I look back at the moment in the art room with the metronome of the carousel marking out the succession of landscapes in the darkened room, I wonder what it was I had 'got' – now that I could no longer see the Freddie Williams' pictures as I once had before, as scratchy marks standing in for something on a background of orange brown.

So my picture records just a doppelganger, and we are left to imagine fruitlessly what would constitute an original: there is no criterion that can distinguish them. Perhaps, then, my image up on the pinboard does record what was out my window that day, that the picture is real or, at least, portrays accurately what I saw out the window when the football commentator called out a high tackle and the opposition now had its chance for a goal.

There are, in the end, a few clues as to what was seen out the window on the way home. The dark wavy streaks in the blue-white sky are a recording of the trees by the side of the road, wattle trees in the foreground between the gravel edge and the paddock fence. Tall, with dark green leaves, their graceful boughs stretching out between each tree, these trees almost disappear, standing so close to me in the car going past at 28 metres a second, and the shutter opening and closing just for that one eighth of a second.

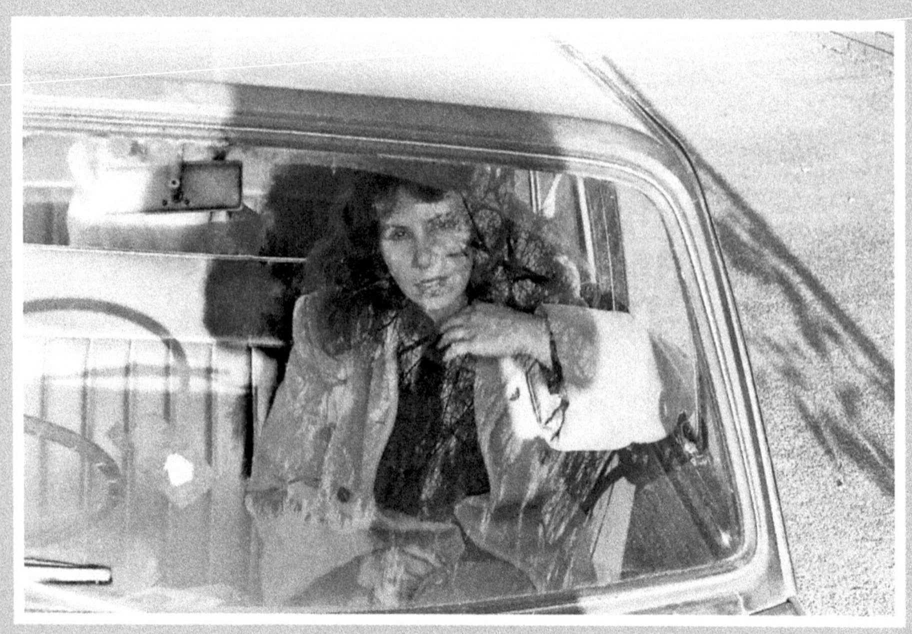

20

Beatrice

This is one of my favourite pictures of Beatrice. I took many pictures of her in the year we first lived together. This picture was taken in August of that year; Beatrice is sitting in the front seat of my car, a Morris 1100, which was parked outside the house. I asked her to stay in the car while I took the pictures through the windscreen. I liked the reflections in the glass and the strong, almost horizontal afternoon sunlight. I remember she was uncomfortable in her full length, double-breasted camel-coloured coat. But she was patient and I took several shots of which I judge this the best.

I first met Beatrice several years earlier when I gave her a lift home in the Morris. At the time I was sharing a half-house with a friend of mine who was attending a school nearby. Beatrice was visiting a teacher colleague who lived in the other half of the house.

I remember Beatrice bundled up in heavy clothing, boots and scarves, her small frame disappearing in all this cold weather gear. We travelled up the mountain in the small car, to where she lived. It was called 'Small House' and it seemed buried in the side of a hill surrounded by thick damp bush. It was very cold. I remember her thanking me for the lift while standing in the doorway to her dark cottage.

The next time I spent any time with Beatrice it was again because I offered her a lift home. This time it was not a one hour drive but a three day journey from one capital city to another.

I was ready to leave and start again in another place. I was leaving my friend with whom I'd been living on the northern shores of this capital city. Beatrice had left Small House and had written off her little car in a bad accident. She had come north to rest and recuperate, staying at the house of her old friend and colleague.

I was headed back to my home city, when I heard that this woman, whom I had met once before, would be happy to share the driving and petrol costs.

She was thirty-one and I was twenty; she had already lived several lives and I was just (if I had known it) on the eve of my second.

My Morris was now nine years old. I had been driving it for three years and it had grown unreliable. Our trip of some 1000 kilometres took three days. The first night was at a truck stop where we slept in the car. In the roadhouse the next morning I left my hat behind. The second night we spent with Bea's family in the country town where they lived. We were warmly greeted by her parents. Her mother said to me "Thank you for bringing my daughter back to me." I also met Bea's dog who was temporarily staying with Bea's parents.

Beatrice was a good driver and I took pictures of her behind the wheel, wearing her steel-rimmed aviator sunglasses. We talked and fashioned a way of being together: she had been a drama teacher at a tertiary institution but had left to write full-time. I had just begun writing prose after an adolescence of poetry. We found our common ground in the books and writers we liked.

On the third night we were close to the city when the car broke down. I managed to get it into a small country town off the highway, where we parked in a field by a little creek. In the morning there was a fog and moving through the grey-white air were horses, snorting streams of steam from their nostrils as they grazed on the damp grass.

Back in the city of my birth most of my friends had left for other parts of the country. So I was slowly caught up in Beatrice's world of former students who were now jugglers and actors, playwrights and drama teachers. We soon found a house to live in, a weatherboard with three bedrooms and a backyard. It was situated in a quiet street in an inner suburb.

After we found the house I got a job nearby for a cabaret and comedy venue. I sat outside in the courtyard peeling and chopping carrots, potatoes, celery, shelling beans and peas, pithing pumpkin and squash.

A former student came to live with us. A budding playwright, he was entranced by Gabriel Garcia Marquez and Antonin Artaud, and immediately suggested setting up stocks in the hallway for periodic self-abasement. He cultivated a moustache and stomped up and down the house with barely suppressed rage and refused to share in any sort of domesticity.

One day Bea's dog came back from the country to stay with us. A Labrador-Alsatian with the markings and narrow snout of an Alsation. A large dog, even as a puppy, she was known as 'Big Dog', though she was named after an old blues musician Beatrice was fond of: Jelly Roll.

The stern young playwright was convinced to swap the idea of the stocks for a chessboard set up in the hallway with a game permanently in progress. We read Flaubert out loud to one another and discussed the latest novel by Patrick White.

Beatrice and I wrote, created a vegetable garden in the small backyard and took the growing dog for regular walks in the park nearby. Big Dog grew very quickly over the months and soon took up the whole of the backseat of the car. In the park I would throw sticks for her which she would race to retrieve and return for another throw.

We were serious, all of us; the atmosphere was one of study; the wine and hallucinogens were like different classrooms in a vast pedagogy. What we read was studied, reviewed, read out and re-read: Castaneda, Freud, Gregory Bateson and Kurt Vonnegut were all picked apart for their contributions to a composite of the world that would make it liveable and perhaps even coherent. And, in all this, no-one was allowed to play a silly move in the ongoing chess games, but take it back and try for something better.

* * *

On the Autumn day I took the series of photos of Bea in the car, the sun was low on the horizon and streaming directly through the windscreen and into Beatrice's eyes. It was difficult getting a shot where she was not squinting or holding a hand up against the Autumn light.

So, for this shot, I have moved directly in front of the car to block the sunlight that is now streaming almost horizontally into the windscreen. Behind me stands the deciduous oak tree whose bare boughs and twigs are reflected on the windscreen. In making my exposure, I have concentrated on Beatrice, allowing either side of the image to bleach out, including the big cuff of her coat. But there is detail – light and shadow, everywhere on the figure bringing her hand to her shirt collar.

There is a white sticker in the centre of the windscreen; it is the remains of the price tag and manufacturer of the new windscreen that replaced one shattered on a recent trip to the seaside. There is no registration sticker on the new windscreen and, to stay within the law, I kept the new registration paper and adhesive label in the glove box.

I have scanned the negative of the original 35mm B&W Tri-X film and can see that the corner of a Melways street directory is just visible on the dashboard.

But there was something here that I had never seen until now. I had wondered why we were in the car on this late afternoon in Autumn. The image is not planned; we were there in the street and I saw the sunlight and the reflections across the windscreen.

On the day I took the picture, I knew exactly how the day had passed. Standing in the street I could feel the sun on my back, knew, without thinking, whether there was a light breeze down the street or if the day had been completely still. I knew intimately the moods and thoughts that had accompanied the hours.

Living through the hours of that day (some forty-seven years ago) I knew what is was that Bea and I had been concerned with; the books we were reading, even the chess move I had made late that morning. And, naturally, I knew exactly what we were doing in the street as the sun drew down the day, and the light came horizontal onto Bea's face through the new windscreen.

But today looking at the photograph taken so long ago, I recall nothing of all that. It is today, this day which is full of the absorbing details, thoughts and sensations that once belonged to the Autumn day so long ago. It is as if that day has become this day; the richness of sensation and the intense experience of being-here that once belonged to that day now belongs to this day: the one in which I write and look at the photograph on the computer screen; the sky, the wind (it is blowing a northerly), the Autumn colours in the garden, the sun still high in the sky on a warm afternoon. I know all this intimately and, belong completely to this day just as once I belonged body and soul, to that far-off day which can only now be re-collected with the aid of a few photographs.

And now, today, I see the dog, the Big Dog, a vague outline in the bleached out darks of the black and white photograph – she is sitting up on the backseat behind where I would sit to drive the car. For, knowing that day as I once did, I knew Big Dog was there;

she was eager to get to the park for her run. But my concern in the photograph was to capture a likeness of Beatrice behind a veil of tracery that, like a fascinator, draws the viewer closer.

Of the dog, for whom we were making the trip a few minutes down the road, we can see almost nothing, just her chest, her head hidden by the roof, but I now see her for the first time, now that I am looking at this photograph, now unable to recollect all that I once knew so intimately. But I see the distinctive octagonal identification disc on the collar around her thickly furred neck. She is there, as she always has been, in that far off Autumn day in this hither-to unexamined photograph of her mistress, Bea. But it is only on this day that I see her for the first time – bereft as I am of that day and all the richness the instinctive belonging that was once mine.

The car has long gone, and so too the dear dog. I still take pictures of Bea. I have another car to visit her in the country where she now lives in a small house with a very active white and ginger terrier called Molly.

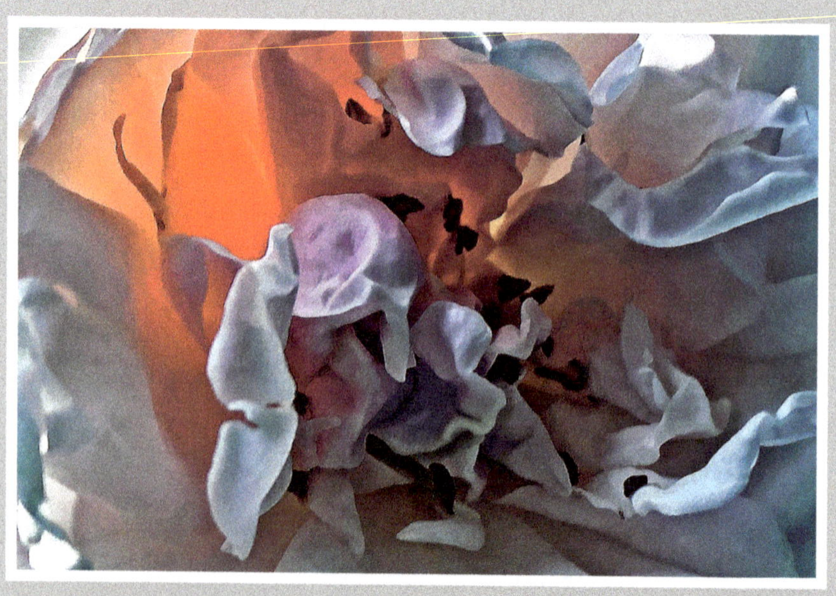

21

The Madame Alfred Carrière Rose

Curled, folded and serrated leaves appear at the ends of straight magenta-coloured twigs on the Japanese maple. Suddenly leaves and buds appear up and down the whippy-droopy branches of the quince. And, in a tight fan of iris leaves, the matt green honed edges spiking away from each other, a single leaf is faintly shadowed with a barely perceptible bulge.

Sepals cap tight-coiled rose petals whose pink is a sliver between the slowly parting green enclosure. Purple spear-tips form along the jointed raspberry canes that I tether loosely to twine strung between wooden stakes.

From the golden elm – still a splay of bare branches and knobbled twigs – sprout the occasional pale-yellow disk that, transparent in the sun, shows its dark seed within.

Against the fence grows an old honeysuckle and a climbing pink scentless rose. In here, over successive years, a blackbird pair nest and raise another generation. This year a magpie took one of the chicks – the sound of the parents was deafening. We chased away the black and white bird from the body on the ground beneath the softly waving yellow honeysuckle. I buried the dead bird. Afterwards the female blackbird sat on the fence not far away from where we sat and seemed unable to go too far a distance from the nest or her absent hatchling.

So spring started: sticky weed sprung between the violets and clambered up the old wood of shrubs. New strands of lilac appeared straight and unobtrusive from the bare earth beneath the Hebe bush and lemon tree.

Everywhere in the garden stems were growing and, as the stem grew from its tip, so around the stem formed the beginnings of leaves. Inside the sepals grew the flowers, tightly bound, the individual petals arranging themselves in various ways: they can be contorted or twisted, folded inwards, or outwards, they can be spirally twisted, they can be open or closed, overlapping or just barely touching one another.

Bright green new leaves march along the growing stem up towards the light, seeking out the heat that Spring seems to promise. It is as if the whole garden is crawling out of the huddle that Winter had once imposed on it.

The photograph is of a Madame Alfred Carrière Rose. It is a climbing rose that I have trained to run horizontally around string tied between two posts on the section of the verandah that can be seen through the work room window. The stems of the rose want to grow straight up and, at this time of year, they push against the underneath of the translucent plastic roof. Periodically I pull them down, wind them around the older canes or the white string itself – run them horizontally from right to left, so they fill the view from the work room through the double glass windows set at waist height which rise almost to the aqua moulding at the junction of wall and ceiling.

The scented rose blooms proliferate, forming the new flowers at the end of each new stem. It has a strong scent that almost has a fizz to it – I call it 'spritzig' – and adds an edge to the soft creamy scent.

* * *

All this intensity in growth comes in many stages, colours and configurations, from the brittle candy-red of the kiss-me-quicks to the pale spade-shaped leaves of the elm to the varying spirals and colours of rose petals. So I was surprised to find the unambiguous and brightly lit fingers of mathematics deep in the thicket of weed, shrub and tree, paring and parsing the stems, leaves, flowers and seeds of everything that grows in the garden.

It seems that leaves arrange themselves on the stem of all plants in only three ways. Most plants, over 80%, arrange their leaves in a spiral pattern going around and up the stem, one after another. Another pattern is that of the roses; the Mde Alfred Carrière rose has leaves placed opposite to one another and so on up the stem, the distichous pattern. The third pattern is the whorl where two or more leaves grow out from the same point of the stem in opposite directions, with the subsequent pair appearing at an angle of 90° to the previous whorl below.

That's it. These three arrangements of leaves around every plant stem is called phyllotaxis. A word made up of two parts, the *phylla* which encompasses not only leaves but seeds, scales and bracts and *taxis* which means arrangement or order. I mention this for the maths that can analyse phyllotaxis also handles other aspects of the spring garden.

We can describe the three patterns of leaf formation as spirals with different offset angles, that is, the angle that separates them on their progression up the growing stem: for most plants the offset angle is 137.5°. The distichous rose has an offset angle of 180° and the whorl is 90°. We can parse the leaves on a stem by counting and turning: the number of leaves counted to find another leaf coming from the same part of the stem, and the number of spiral turns it takes to reach this leaf sitting directly above the lower leaf. The two numbers are *always* a pair of successive Fibonacci numbers. And this is true for all phyla taxiing for position on a growing plant stem.

The Fibonacci sequence is a simple succession of numbers following just one rule: add the previous two numbers to form the next number.

$$0,1,1,2,3,5,8,13,21,34,55,\ldots$$

The number of petals of most flowers is also a Fibonacci number. The picture of the Mde Alfred Carrière rose shows a wash of petals and it is true the flower has a rather 'informal' shape. But I did take one bloom apart and found the total number of variously-sized petals was 89 petals, the next Fibonacci number in the sequence above.

After the blackbirds lost their chick and had stopped haunting the place of their loss they seemed to vanish. But one day I was passing between the Mde Alfred Carrière rose and the window of the work room and I felt I was being watched. So I stopped and turned towards the rose where at eye level sat the female blackbird staring at me. I froze and saw that it sat in a new nest, tucked in amongst the lateral canes of the plant and sheltered above by the gutter of the verandah roof. I averted my eyes and walked quietly, quickly away.

Fibonacci numbers turn up in more complicated spirals such as those describing the form of seed heads in sunflowers, and the scales of pine cones or petals in some more formally shaped roses. Pine cone scales have many spirals moving in opposite directions but again, counting the number of spirals, we find they are successive numbers in the Fibonacci sequence.

When we divide two Fibonacci numbers, say those of our leaves on a stem and the turns to reach the leaf directly above, or the numbers of spirals on a pinecone we get a ratio that soon settles down to a value 1.618043. This is an irrational number because it has no end, the digits to the right of the decimal point go on forever and do not settle into repetition. This ratio is also called the golden ratio and seems intimately related to the Fibonacci sequence whose numbers can be used to create squares and rectangles that grow in size but retain the golden ratio that relate the sides of the geometric forms.

I am reaching the limit of my mathematical understanding so will not go on enumerating the connection between the Fibonacci sequence and the golden ratio. But I want to pick up on an earlier mention of the offset of leaves on a stem. In most plants this is an angle of precisely 137.5°. It turns out that this is the golden ratio expressed as an angle. So the 'use' of Fibonacci numbers in nature is partly to generate this offset angle. The value of all this mathematics to plants is that it provides optimal access to sunlight and moisture to leaves, and optimal packing of other phyla such as seeds in a seed head, scales, and bracts.

In the case of seeds, optimal means that each seed has the same amount of space around it as every other seed; mathematical modelling generating 'seeds' in a circle using different offset angles show that these other arrangements are not nearly as space-efficient.

Looking back at the photograph of the Mde Alfred Carrière rose there is little evidence of maths in the swirl of line and colour making up my picture of the rose's corolla. The black bits arranged roughly in the centre are anthers, the tips of stamens from which the pollen is released. This rose is known as a French Antique rose and was bred, artificially selected, by Joseph Schwartz in 1879. He named his new cultivar after the wife of the editor of *Revue Horticole*, Madame Alfred Carrière.

My image is a 'photographic cultivar', and like any rose breeder I have selected various features I want to keep through successive generations using my image editor. I have discarded traits that do not suit my taste; there is no background or context to my flower, the colours are generated through successive tweaking of various settings so that they no longer resemble those I started out with. I have increased the 'informality' of the petal arrangement to suggest something chaotic but rhythmic, my rule not so much the Darwinian one fitting the organism to its environment but rather creating something abstract though still retaining sufficient aspects that will identify the original object.

Which brings us to the question of why and how plants utilise the Fibonacci sequence to guide and control growth. Few writers I read on the topic mention evolution explicitly and, if they do, have a hazy notion of evolutionary theory.

Other writers focus on the how, and look to theories based on geometry or chemical factors, and most invoke terms like 'spooky' or 'magical' to describe the regularities and relations between the Fibonacci numbers, the golden ratio, and their expression in phyllotaxis.

Evolution is a messy business. It has no strategy, it does not consider the future nor 'learn' from past 'mistakes' – it is orientated to nothing in particular, so to speak of 'optimisation' and 'efficiency' in this context is a bit misleading. It is a natural process – it is the natural process; evolution is what we mean when we say nature. Ad hoc, haphazard and short-term; but not random and not unconstrained. It is conservative, it will keep what works and will draw again on what has proven beneficial in terms of the reproductive success of the organism.

I think this is sufficient to account for the success of plants and their utilisation of the seemingly few number of phyllotactic strategies we see: it works, plants grow, leaves find a position where they can photosynthesise enough and stems can channel water to the base of the plant. Seeds grow and find a place on the growing seed head maximally packed. And the numbers? It is we who find the numbers and the ratios. Mathematicians and scientists say the language of the universe is mathematics, and sometimes I think what is meant is that maths generates the universe, its laws, constraints, and the numbers. Other times I hear that the universe is only explicable with the use of mathematics. I think human beings are language animals, and that the regularities, patterns, and responses to environments in the world are there for such an animal to find.

We are creatures who are uncomfortable with the lack of pattern, fall sick without regularities and repetition, and whose desire for meaning is so overwhelming that its absence is another name for death.

The laws and mathematics we find, we have need of; plants need rather sunlight, moisture, soil and a way to reproduce. The natural world is not 'spooky' not 'magical', these are other words we use in our compulsive desire for meaning.

Sitting here I see out the window to where the blackbird nest sits almost invisible in the canes and stems and leaves of the Mde Alfred Carrière rose. The blackbird pair have been incubating five blue speckled eggs. One day I went out to have a look and found two dead chicks on the verandah. They were barely out of their shells, indeed one chick lay half inside the broken egg.

Since then we have heard the scraping of claws of the predatory magpies on the plastic verandah roof and shooed them away each time with a broom struck on the underneath of the roof. But two eggs have hatched in the nest and both parents work in tandem bringing worms and other invertebrates to feed the new hatchlings.

I have been in the garden noting the phyllotaxis and Fibonacci divergence: counting leaves and turns on the Mde Alfred Carrière rose, distichous, 3 leaves and 2 turns. Apple tree, spiral, 3 leaves and 2 turns. Blackberry, spiral, 5 leaves and 3 turns. Lilac, whorl, 3 leaves and 2 turns. Euphorbia, spiral, 5 leaves and 3 turns. Garlic, whorl, 2 leaves and 1 turn.

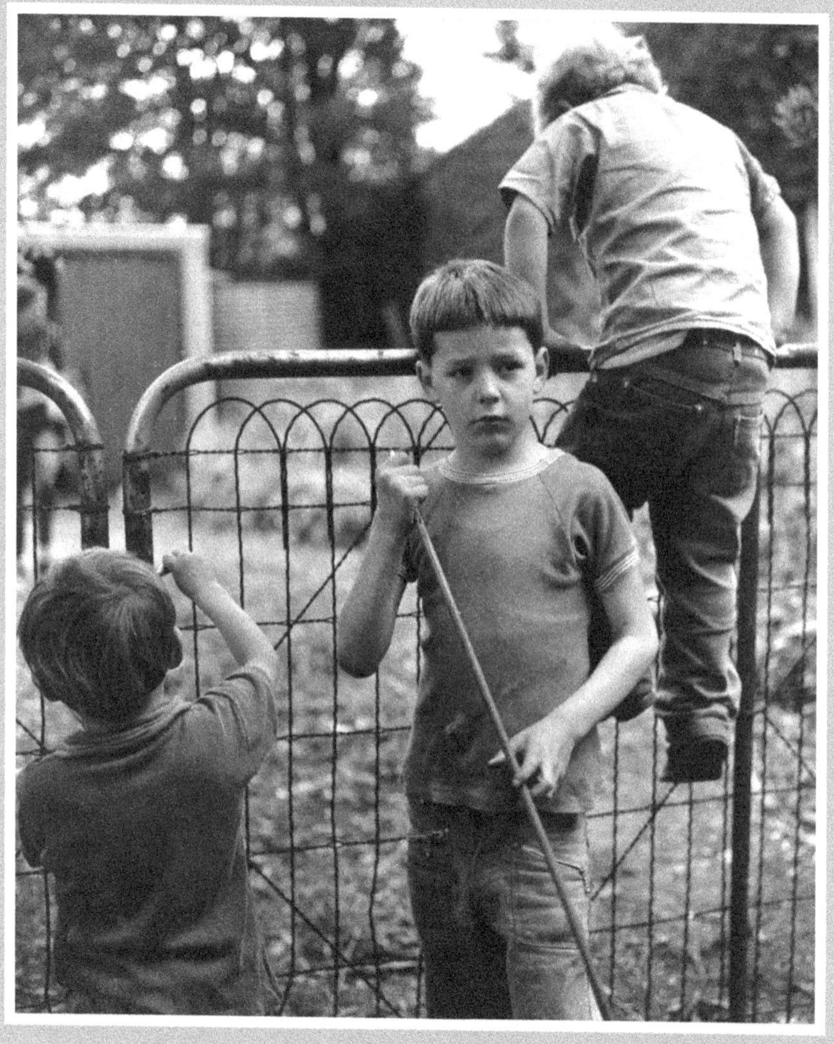

22

The Gate

Oh I recognise this. The red shirt, crew cut neckline, each sleeve edged by three white bands, the cloth very soft, a favourite top. Yes, and underneath is a very white singlet of a rougher weave but still soft on the skin. We all wore these singlets and, if we took off our shirts, we had also to take off the white singlets as well.

It is a maroon red and I know the soft feel of the often washed cotton well. I know the gentle press on my skin, just above the collar bone, where the stitch runs, joining the banded edging to the rest of the top. I know the fit, the feel of deep colour, the light touch of the sleeves around my arms.

And the stick: cobbled together from a piece of bamboo, some dowel, and tipped with a brass ferrule from a discarded umbrella. It serves all purposes, fulfils all intents, it is light and perfectly straight and untouchable by any other hand.

The jeans with their slanting pocket openings, the individual zips attached to the bobbled chains; one open and the other closed up, the contents unseen and unknown to all. Like the top, a favourite pair of trousers: the cloth torn away exposes the left knee, not sewable, not to be discarded, but worn up here in the mountains, on the block.

A steep forest block, the long straight bodies of felled mountain ash lie across the ground; the round, smooth trunks still tower over us as we struggle through the crushed and broken undergrowth around the cut down trees: thin-limbed stringy barks, box and ferns still growing thickly, tangling together.

We are brothers at the gate; one climbs, arms flexing, keeping the body steady, hands gripping the top rail; another delicately lifts the steel latch from its bed, freeing the two halves of the gate to swing apart enough to pass through.

I am holding the pointy end of my stick, the cool brass between finger and palm, looking out, back the way we've come, the gravel road set about by the push of the forest that we're here to clear, to bare the block, so my uncle can build my grandmother, Sassafras Gran, a house to live in.

I know the smell of the wet red earth, am alert to the creak of the tall ash high above where the wind tugs and pulls, spinning loose scented leaves through the trembling stems, branches, falling silently on the black lines of ants carrying cut litter across the ground.

I hear the drip of water, a single drop, a singular water fall, drop from leaf to lower leaf. The faint tap of slippery contact before another silent drop; all repeated softer and softer as the forest marches away, upright, on the tilting sides of the mountain.

It is the summer holidays of 1964–1965, Sassafras Gran has come down to don thick gloves and wide brimmed hat and walk among the snakes and spiders, call to the kookaburras, and pull bracken, gorse and weeds from the ground around the fallen timber of ash and box gum. We are all here to help, say mother and father; frowning at us with the exertion of it all.

But I know, looking out, that there is nothing known here and everything must be searched out and looked at anew; no place is ever the same twice and all exploration is to find what has never been found before.

Sassafras Gran works as a housekeeper in a big house on a great property called Yarrum Park. She lives there, cooks the meals, feeds the chooks, and cleans the rooms. Today we all meet here, go through the gate behind me, once my brothers have opened the wire and metal.

I recognise all of this. The scratch running on the underside of my right arm does not come from working on the block; it is just days old, the series of small punctures are still red, they mark the passage of the stiff pointed hedge stem as it runs the length of my forearm. I feel the tightness sometimes, the skin not so elastic as the scab forms. I am deep inside the dense cypress hedge that forms the boundary between our front yard and the busy road outside.

Working my way further into its green pungent furrowed light and dark self, hollowing out a new space. My brothers are burrowing further into the unbroken wood; we are all playing some unformed game, heedless of the cuts and scratches which perhaps, in the end, form the only rules to this strange and hazardous game.

I rub the brass ferrule knowing it will have *its* work cut out today. It will both mark what is seen, and create what it is to be found; unbidden and unheralded the block waits our depredations, the cry of discovery and accident.

Yesterday's scratches and blood do not count.

Inside the wooden garage on the block are the truncated, foreshortened and abbreviated parts of a complete house; a sink with no stand, power points and no wall, electric wires and cords hang among the spider webs and strands of vine. Tins of petrol and kerosene form their own corner of shiny tin and rusted metal. Is that carpet on the ground, heaving and mounding, falling away as the dirt softens and hardens beneath? Or is it just compacted dirt of the forest floor glossy with use and crumbling with roots where the gaps appear at all the joins of this distraught house?

The air in here seems to suck up our voices; we all sound unlike ourselves; we whisper undone syllables that disappear into the shadows where I do not want to go; places far from the centre of things.

But we drink tea and there are biscuits, Sassafras Gran insists we are all workers and we need tea and biscuits for our labours. Here she is not a housekeeper; here is not a house yet.

I am looking out, I feel the cool on my bare knee when the air rises from the damp red earth; the creak of the tall ash reminding me, startling me into a recognition, that they are alive and their green wood rubs against itself like sinew, as the wind, stronger even than them, makes them sway, bend bodies hundreds of feet high and many feet wide where they grow out of the soil.

Later I will crawl inside the stump of one of these trees; it has been sawn and then, when the enormous weight has become hinged by the woodsmen's saws, it has fallen, pulling fibre from fibre, leaving a jagged split taller than me and my brothers who will, one by one, lower ourselves into the rotted out centre of the stump.

Sassafras Gran sets fires, rakes up torn bush, brush and bracken, bunches newspaper and strikes sulphur to set it alight. She stands there holding the end of the rake, resting as the sweet smoke crackles and wreathes about the oily leaves and wet fronds. Everywhere there are small mounds, breathing orange fire, for we are clearing the block; those that look after us have rakes and spades to pull embers together, and cut fire breaks in the dirt.

We walk in and out of grey blue smoke as we explore, following invisible suggestions, picking up unknown scents and calling out one anther lost briefly in drifts of smoke, in the directions and instructions of mother and father and Sassafras Gran.

Oh yes, I recognise all this; staring out, full of everything that is to happen, silently alive to all that has already happened; the accidents of birth, the corollaries of consanguinity, the press of DNA and the unbidden thoughts and the words to express them; the notation of the rules, the great happenstance that closes my eyes at the end of each day; the simple patterns that once drawn can only be played out again in all variations possible.

The scar on the inside of my left arm, a dark nick in the pale skin; the outcome of being chased by my father around the Hills Hoist set in the back yard. He wields the unsheathed scalpel, almost invisible in his big hand, "Don't be ridiculous!", is his cry, then and now. Around we run, one after the other. I reach up and set the square of wire and metal spinning on its axis. "It won't hurt!". But it did, the splinter is fast under the skin, blood and puss pushing, pushing at the obdurate sliver of wood. The clothes line squeaks and creaks, unoiled and unused. But it all came out as it seldom does.

So today we are at the gate, soon it will be opened and the block will be cleared, fires will be lit, the adults will walk and talk, throw out their arms to point, or shade their eyes. I will hold my stick vertical upon the ground, and go out with my brothers who have come through the gate with me, go out and see what can be found, what might make sense, what can be salvaged from the clearing block.

Wakefield Press is an independent publishing and
distribution company based in Adelaide, South Australia.
We love good stories and publish beautiful books.
To see our full range of books, please visit our website at
www.wakefieldpress.com.au
where all titles are available for purchase.
To keep up with our latest releases, news and events,
subscribe to our monthly newsletter.

Find us!

Facebook: www.facebook.com/wakefield.press
Instagram: www.instagram.com/wakefieldpress